Journey to Success

Journey to Success

Navigating the Treacherous Slopes of Working with a Variety of People

Steven A. DiStefano

ROWMAN & LITTLEFIELD
Lanham • Boulder • New York • London

Published by Rowman & Littlefield
An imprint of The Rowman & Littlefield Publishing Group, Inc.
4501 Forbes Boulevard, Suite 200, Lanham, Maryland 20706
www.rowman.com
86-90 Paul Street, London EC2A 4NE, United Kingdom

Copyright © 2022 by Steven A. DiStefano

All rights reserved. No part of this book may be reproduced in any form or by any electronic or mechanical means, including information storage and retrieval systems, without written permission from the publisher, except by a reviewer who may quote passages in a review.

British Library Cataloguing in Publication Information Available

Library of Congress Cataloging-in-Publication Data Available

ISBN 978-1-4758-6550-9 (cloth)
ISBN 978-1-4758-6551-6 (pbk.)
ISBN 978-1-4758-6552-3 (electronic)

For my mother, Ann DiStefano; my late father, Frank; my children, Ryan and Nick; and all the educators who work tirelessly to help shape tomorrow's leaders.

Contents

Preface ix

Introduction xv

Chapter 1: Keep Your Teachers Current 1

Chapter 2: Build and Maintain Trust 13

Chapter 3: Build Community 25

Chapter 4: Think outside the Box 33

Chapter 5: Be Empathetic and Compassionate 43

Chapter 6: Believe in the Magic of Every Child Every Day 53

Chapter 7: Building Atlantian Fields School District 63

Chapter 8: Creators of Our Universe: Adopt and Adapt 81

Bibliography 87

Preface

On an otherwise drab and uneventful early spring hump day, my slow and methodical postdinner descent into prepping the kids for the next morning was interrupted by a text from an old friend. He alerted me to the fact that it was National *Twilight Zone* Day. Being an avid fan of the legendary series—which came to being, peaked, and died temporarily before I was even born—I was naturally curious, and unequivocally enthused. I didn't know what it meant, but it sounded like it was right up my alley.

I immediately envisioned myself in a deep, mesmerized, catatonic state in the tattered living room chair, sipping down soft drinks and devouring leftovers. *The Twilight Zone* Marathon Day had been, and still is, one of the few times of the year when I'm glued to the television set for more than an hour. So, like every other being of this earth and beyond, I began googling National *Twilight Zone* Day.

I was led to sites that took us back in time to a remote paradise somewhere in the outskirts of TV land. Others provided unique ideas, like a time traveler coming back from seventy-five years into the future to tell us how to enjoy life now before the pending technological apocalypse destroys humankind as we know it. There was even a site here and there that catered to true enthusiasts who had just saddled up, rented a Feederwarg, and prepared for their mission to track down and capture something as entertaining and addictive as Serling's masterpiece. Feederwargs, by the way, were bred during the early stages of the third millennia by her majesty's colonial guard to ward off the evil spirits conjured up by domestic rebels after the Midnight Wars.

After putting my eyes and fingers through a workout, I reflected on some of my most cherished *Twilight Zone* memories. The first one to come to mind was from my early twenties. I stayed home one New Year's Eve, when the annual marathon first started airing. My mom lay on one couch, and I, on the other. Every now and then, she would take a break to go up to the kitchen and make us both a snack. Listening to her laugh and reminisce about being scared out of her wits while seeing some of the episodes as a young woman on her family's first and only television set personalized the night and brought Mr. Serling—and the past—right into our living room.

But my most treasured memory isn't the nostalgia of my parents' finished basement or of the time when I tried to argue with a college friend about time travel indeed being possible if one could traverse space at the speed of light. No. I placed my phone down on the arm of the living room chair face first, gave the otherwise anxious dog a snack that would last him no less than an hour, and hustled to eighth-period reading class.

Mrs. McGuiness was her name. East Middle School. Binghamton, New York. 1986. I scurried to finish a couple more math problems and cross them off my assignment pad so that I had less to take home. I had just passed by a half-dozen friends whose names had slipped my mind.

It was eighth period. Eighth grade. The last class of the day on a beautiful spring afternoon. What was I going to do when I got home? It didn't matter. I couldn't wait for that otherwise ominous bell to ring. I felt like my cat, Domino, who would magically appear every time my dad turned the can opener on.

The theme for reading class was "Short Stories," and "Science Fiction" was the unit for the month. Most kids took it like they had taken a sick day for a slight headache, swallowing hard and pretending not to like the cherry-flavored medicine that Mom had from the last visit to the doctor. A select few took the serial killer approach, saying nothing at all, but one look into their cold eyes revealed an uninhibited passion to drive a stake straight through the heart of the textbook in front of them. To me, it was more than a series of boring assignments handed out like telephone numbers at a middle school dance just to find out who read the story. It was the best unit of study ever. And it's what got me interested in reading and school at a crucial time in my life.

We read stories like "The Ruum" by Arthur Porges and "An Occurrence at Owl Creek Bridge" by Ambrose Bierce. We acted out plays and watched a couple of original *Twilight Zone* episodes. I was fascinated, enthralled. I had only read one other time in my life on my own. Otherwise, stick me into a "high" reading group, and I'll read all the words you put in front of me but won't remember any of them.

As we read through a small variety of sci-fi shorts, I eagerly anticipated that twisted ending and aha moment that always put a smile on my face and helped me think of a good story to share with Mom during the family dinner at 5:30. Science fiction sparked an interest in me that I had never before realized, except for when playing with my *Star Wars* action figures years earlier.

Like everything else those days, that interest came and went like the girls passing in the hallway. It was quickly followed by a pentathlon of boring classes, blossoming and dying friendships, and an occasional sneaking out of my parents' house to meet some friends for a night's worth of shenanigans.

Before long, college came and went, and I returned to a place where the man whom I had learned about eight or nine years earlier called home: Binghamton, New York. About one year later, I secured a position teaching high school social studies. It was in a quiet bedroom community, lying between a stretch of highway in rusted-out Upstate New York that had just sent out an SOS signal and the far reaches of scattered barns and eerie cemeteries. It was one of the last remaining regional fortresses standing strong against the onslaught of NAFTA and an exodus of a working middle class into the leaf-covered trails of Oblivion.

It wasn't a hot spot, thriving with young professionals looking to start families and buy townhouses on Teacup Lane. It wasn't a booming metropolis, riddled with new high rises and manicured lobbies. However, it was home, and it was packed with droves of potential Rod Serlings eager to learn and forge ahead into the next phase of their lives.

I soon realized that some of those "radical"-thinking college professors actually had quite a few good pointers for their future educators. Making learning fun and entertaining was just the beginning of best teaching practices. Constructivism. Reading for a purpose. Outcomes-based standards. We were on our way to excellence long before No Child Left Behind and the Common Core invaded like a school of hovering saucers threatening to land on Manhattan's Upper East Side.

That creative spirit of teaching—trying out new deliveries, getting fast and meaningful feedback every Monday through Friday nearly every hour of the day, reading and studying feverishly just to stay a step ahead of our students, and fostering a community of synthesis and creation—is what drives the best in the business. It's also what drives the best leaders in the business.

Success comes and goes, like the ghosts of fallen Civil War heroes in isolated corners of forgotten battlefields. Likewise, successful educational leaders come and go. But success doesn't have to depend on the fortune or misfortune of the three wishes granted by the genie who came out of that flask found at Antiqueville's garage sale or Mr. Shiner's Warehouse. Rather, successful leaders can lead their schools into the vastness of success by employing certain strategies and taking on team leader characteristics that help them build relationships with their employees and their community. But even more vital to a school administrator's success is the ability to be just one cog in the wheel of a quality leadership team.

Inherent in every successful school is an environment conducive to learning. For those of us schooled in schooling sometime after 1980 in the Madeline Cheek Hunter approach to teaching, one of the essential elements of any successful lesson plan is an objective. What is the purpose of the lesson, and how are students going to demonstrate their ability to do or know what they've been taught? The same philosophy can be applied to schools. The purpose is clear. Or is it? How do we know that our children have fully achieved the outcomes we are looking for? One strategy that allows all stakeholders to assess program results is to create clear, relevant, attainable, and measurable goals that define academic success for their organization.

What is the graduation rate? What percentage of students are passing final exams? Who is going to what colleges after high school? How do the test scores of elementary, middle, and high schoolers compare to those of their peers in other similar districts? Good leadership teams take the lead in developing, communicating, and focusing on such goals throughout the school year and beyond. The goals drive the decisions, program analyses, faculty meetings, master schedules, and everything else affiliated with teamwork in every school in any district.

The whole concept of fostering a goal-oriented organization can be controversial. Ultimately in a school, however, not having goals generally means that there is no way to define success. Or there is no reason to move beyond what is already getting done. The real controversies surface when it comes to how to go about meeting those goals. It's throughout those trials and tribulations where sound leadership skills, which focus on driving the larger team forward, are as vital to success as care and upkeep are to your underground potassium garden (common now in the backwoods of Pacific islands but coming soon to a developed world near you).

Unfortunately, however, several school administrators have met fates similar to some of the more shadowy figures found in the timeless scenes of *The Twilight Zone*: ruin and despair. The difference? In education, they could have been avoided. Far too often, good leaders believe that they have to be the begin all and end all of their organization. Quite the contrary is true. Very few people, even organizational leaders, have a plethora of skills so sharp that Poseidon could edge the points of his trident with them. Rather, like the front earwing on your favorite raptorball team, the most effective leaders use their best skills in conjunction with the skills of their teammates to bring the organization into the future.

Whether you lead a small rural district or a large urban one, take center stage in a modern progressive building or a classic traditional one, or are preparing for that next chapter in life or just starting out, these leadership lessons, taken from the "dimension not only of sight and sound but of mind," are at the core of my educational philosophy and have undoubtedly helped administrative teams effectively navigate the treacherous trails of adversity.

They are not unique in the sense of being so secretive that they're locked in a CIA-issued trunk zapped through time and snuck into the middle wagon of an 1800s Wells Fargo convoy. They do, however, contain subtle, barely visible doors, large and accessible enough for even a cloned wooly mammoth to trudge through.

So, sit back, fasten your seat belt, and relax. You are about to embark on a short journey through time and space. Your destination: Atlantian Fields Central School District. Purpose: to establish yourself as an effective leader of a universe-class educational community. Methodology: get to know the other passengers who just boarded the flight back to an area that was once known as one of the millions of scenic bypasses on earth. Learn from their triumphs and their mistakes, figure out what strategies should and should not be employed, and build a team.

The other passengers themselves won't speak to you. But with your newly enhanced, self-activated telepathic brain matter expansion chip, you will know their stories. Some are teachers, some are administrators, and some are just people who spent at least a portion of their life in the *Twilight Zone*. Each one of them has a story. Those stories each hold a lesson, a lesson that will put you in the new transcripts of Atlantian Fields history. What you take away from your fellow trailblazers will help you settle into your new community and survive everything from homecoming weekend to the long frigid winters and postprom party. But none of it can be done alone.

Introduction

Sil was just a child when his dad first brought him there. They had everything he had imagined and more. The aisles were as bright as the star-dusted midnight sky and longer than the commuter train they'd ride when heading into town for ball games. On every shelf there was something different: the first laser printer ever created, an exact replica of Neil Armstrong's boots, a natural-born Siamese cat. Every time they went, the oldest items would intrigue them just as much as the newest ones.

One day they would head over to the "Freedom Ring" section; the next, it would be "The Last of the Tyrants." People from all over town and throughout the country would come every Saturday morning. Two lines would form right outside the gate, meander through the parking lot, and curl onto the sidewalk out front.

There was never a dull moment when visiting Mr. Shiner's Warehouse. Sil even had his first crush there. Her name was Monica. She had long brown hair, sparkling green eyes, and two huge front teeth that took center stage every time she talked. They both "got lost" one Saturday afternoon while his father and her mother engaged in some small talk over an octopus that Mr. Shiner had converted into a table.

They disappeared into the nearby aisles, gasping at the microscopic organisms in the petri dishes and giggling a little at the more gruesome displays. It was just enough to distract them from that awkward moment when they'd reach for each other's hands. She'll forever stick with Sil, no matter how far away she is now.

The same goes for Mr. Shiner's place. He opened a few years before Sil was able to go and truly understand the miracles that he had preserved in the vacated airplane plant. As Sil grew up, he read about Mr. Shiner's ventures. Apparently, he had purchased the plant sometime after the Subterranean Uprising. He started small, salvaging "missing" items from abandoned museums and bartering homegrown veggies for garage-stored antiques.

After the war had shifted overseas and things returned to normal, admission picked up. Soon, he outgrew his place and secured a loan to expand into the plant where he still stands today. Between Sil, his father, and his son, they've probably visited a few dozen times and bought hundreds of historical items dating back thousands of years or more.

"So, what'll it be today, son? A ride on the Super Deluxe Mixer Fixer? A couple of tickets to Beg and Sniff's Pauper Show?"

"Thanks, Mr. Shiner, but no. We're doing something a little different today. We're just going to walk around and see as much as we can. When the time is right and something more affordable catches our eyes, we'll let you know," said Sil.

"OK. Well, that doesn't sound *too* crazy."

"No, but this will probably be our last visit for quite some time."

"Quite some time? I don't think I like the sound of that," Mr. Shiner replied.

Sil let out a heavy sigh, held back his emotions, and shared the news. "We're leaving tomorrow, Mr. Shiner."

"Vacation, son?" he asked.

"Unfortunately, not exactly." Sil looked down at his son and saw himself as a ten-year-old boy looking up to his own father twenty-five years earlier. Sil had to turn away before his swelling eyes became too obvious. Mr. Shiner's silence made them swell up even more. Sil gulped down as much trepidation as he could and gathered whatever guts he had left. "We're moving, Mr. Shiner."

"You're moving?" Mr. Shiner looked as if Sil and his son had just landed in his lobby from another galaxy. His jaw dropped in disbelief. He then shuffled his eyes between the two of them, waiting impatiently for Sil to explain when, where, and why.

"Over to Atlantian Fields."

"Atlantian Fields?" Mr. Shiner's astonishment came to a screeching halt and took a ninety-degree turn as he comforted Sil with a proud snicker and a cocking back of his skinny head. His glowing white hair waved gently behind him as he thrusted up his bifocals and tapped the wooden counter with his wedding band. His whole intention was to suck up those tears before they rolled down Sil's cheeks and into his son's hair.

"We just can't do it anymore. Money is tight. There just aren't any more opportunities here."

"You got a job lined up, do ya'?" he asked.

"I don't. But they're practically giving the land away."

"They tried that before, you know. Didn't work out really well for some of them."

"You certainly do know your history, Mr. Shiner. No one will ever argue with you on that."

"No. I guess they wouldn't. Be careful though. Interplanetary travel can be awfully costly these days. And did I hear that the fields are all cleaned up?"

"Yes. I believe you may have heard that. We've done our research, Mr. Shiner. The fields are all free of nuclear fallout, plutonium, all traces of the carcinogens that nearly wiped out the entire planet."

"What about the villages? The natives?"

"Fortunately, the last of the chartered ones were wiped out no less than five or six years ago. They say there might be some scattered ones around and maybe some small nomadic herds, but they're not very confident about their survival skills. And more likely than not, they're inland quite a way, far from the land we're redeveloping."

"Well, son, I wish you the best of luck. Your father would be proud of you. He was a good man, and you're following in his footsteps. I knew that the minute you first walked in with Junior here. And if you find something that catches your eye, any one of them, and it's not too, too much, go ahead and bring it with you. Take it back to its rightful spot. Right down to earth.

"Despite their flaws, we mustn't forget that their technology and drive to succeed is why we stand with our own three feet on this soil today. It's hard to imagine being that far removed, but generations ago, all it took was one earthling with one so-called outlandish idea. I just hope we can continue to learn from their mistakes."

"I hope so, Mr. Shiner. I really hope so. Thank you for everything. You take care, Mr. Shiner. I'll let you know what we find."

Chapter 1

Keep Your Teachers Current

Passenger 1A is a slight man. His glasses are as fixed on his face as a mailbox post is on an old country road. His reach: slightly longer than his flannel sleeves can stretch. He still roams about dimly lit hallways, holding onto his shiny red apple along with the coffee mug that his favorite student purchased for him some time ago for Christmas. He minds his own business; is generally pleasant; and rarely, if ever, speaks up about anything at all having to do with the building's climate and culture.

His neighbor, Passenger 1B, is no stranger to him. In fact, the two often travel together and have been friends for quite some time. It was a friendship that blossomed from a collegial relationship at Steel Sanity High School in Acorn Fields, Missouri.

You see, Passenger 1B used to be the principal there, and Passenger 1A was one of his most respectful—and silent—faculty members. Prior to boarding this flight, each of them shared a serving of mashed Aquatic Blue Rabbit with Passengers 1C and 1D. Little did they realize that the four of them had something in common: They were all rendered obsolete before boarding Flight 607.

Passenger 1C once found himself traversing one of the murky lanes of *The Twilight Zone*.[1] He was there alongside his leader, Passenger 1D. Both of them experienced a fate that none of us could empathize with, for Passenger 1C is Mr. Romney Wordsworth. It was here in this other dimension, where he was brought to trial by none other than Passenger 1D, the Chancellor. Luckily for us, footage from that trial has been preserved.

Mr. Romney Wordsworth, a librarian, was declared "obsolete" by the State. His thoughts, his beliefs, even his occupation—all restricted by a futuristic dictatorship that had stripped humanity of the essential elements of liberty and progress. There are no more books. There is no more God.

This is from *The Twilight Zone*. It's 1961, season 2. Mr. Serling has just brought the harsh realities of America's most feared enemy, communism, into our very own living rooms. There's no way that anyone watching could grasp living in such fear: in a functioning society, complete with law and order yet riddled with oppression. Automatons supporting a representative of a dictatorial government whose only ounce of compassion lies with several attempts to get Mr. Wordsworth to retract his statement—that he is indeed a librarian—for fear of elimination at the hands of the State.

This *Twilight Zone* classic came like all, on the heels of the red scare of the 1950s. The Korean conflict, Senator McCarthy, satellites into orbit, and a left-wing onslaught to overthrow a racial divide as old as the nation itself. It was a time of change, uncertain change. Sparing the details of just one of Mr. Serling's masterpieces, the viewer in this instance is left with an ending that promises neither doom nor consolation. The villain, the Chancellor himself, ironically meets what's coming to him, and one could assume that someone else will eventually come to power.

Aside from the all too familiar pitfalls of authoritarian leadership, there are other lessons that can be pulled from this story. Mr. Wordsworth, it appears, hasn't adjusted with the times, just like Passenger 1A. But to our dismay, nearly everyone else has—*nearly* being the operative word. Wordsworth is charged and found guilty of being a librarian. Based on the Chancellor's own words and the council's vote, he is rendered obsolete.

It appears that the Chancellor himself, however, has also failed to adjust with the times. Like most Americans of the time could imagine, the members of this dictatorial society do not appear to be scared of the Chancellor. No member of the council judging Mr. Wordsworth casts any doubt on anything that they are doing. The people do not fear because they have become the fear. They are part of a suppressive system: simply put, an arm of the Chancellor with whom they render obsoleteness. When the Chancellor himself breaks the norm and steps out of the inner circle of fear, he himself ironically is also rendered obsolete and set to be exterminated.

Truth being told, similar situations occur in our schools today. Some teachers are quiet, peaceful, mild-mannered sorts of creatures who desire the comfort of their own desk chairs and laptop computers. They'll pick up their heads with a smile, say hello, and find their cups of coffee before grabbing their two thousand copies of mimeographed dittos off the seldom-used, nearly outdated machine in the most secluded retired hallways of the building.

They don't rock the boat, have a core group of common supporters in each other, and very rarely raise the ire of anyone who makes a second career out of complaining about the lack of this or that in the building. Because of their complacency, they are often well liked by their colleagues and supervisors.

When Passenger 1A transposed himself into a new room this past school year, he quickly picked up the old habits that he had left behind in the more remote room, which still bore the putrid green from the "new" paint job done against his will in '89. Students liked him, as did parents, the principal, and building staff. He was the type who really got into history and spent an exorbitant amount of time on the Age of Exploration.

Parents would come to open house and tell each other about doing the same hand-drawn maps of misshapen continents that their kids were now doing and reminisce about his tales of sited mermaids and sea dragons the size of Tyrannosaurus rexes. This, they did when they had him "back in the good ol' days." He was very well versed in this topic, and everyone knew it—because he did the same thing year after year after year. In fact, every fifteen to eighteen months or so, a new rumor of his immortality would come and go, as people insisted that he must've lived with the explorers during the 1500s.

He earned his impeccable evaluations as well as his stellar rapport with students. Every year at around the end of May, he would receive an "authentic" letter from the senior class president inviting him to be one of their distinguished guest teachers at the annual graduation ceremony. He would humbly oblige, and his name would again be etched into the program with an asterisk noting that he had been recognized more than twenty times.

His principal, Passenger 1B, gleefully announces the senior class "favorites" at the end-of-year faculty "meeting" over a catered breakfast. As always, everyone claps and laughs when the explorer's name is called, and the fearless leader always asks, "How many years is this now?" even though he knows the answer.

All of this is celebratory until the very last week, that is, when final exam scores are released and those who had Passenger 1A didn't exactly knock it out of the park. With the rookie teachers, the principal sends an ominous "Please see me" e-mail and then makes them sit in his office, one scoot away from a chair full of hot grilled cheese sandwiches fresh off the griddle.

But *they* need to learn. They should do better. The explorer, however, we know that he's good. The kids just didn't have it together for the exam this year. Last year, they didn't study hard enough. And the year before that? Well, those kids were just immature—the whole class. Rather than digging a little, looking for gaps in the explorer's delivery, or simply having an uncomfortable conversation with him, the principal simply lets it go until the following year. Eventually, he knows, that the explorer will soon enter into the parallel dimension known as retirement and say goodbye to his two million supporters from years past.

Unfortunately for Mr. Wordsworth the librarian, this was not the direction in which the Chancellor went. No. The Chancellor eliminated Mr. Wordsworth and had absolutely no hesitation in doing so. Certainly, such educational leaders as Passenger 1B aren't rendering people like the explorer obsolete through a dictator's inner circle of henchmen like the Chancellor did to Romney Wordsworth. Nor are they forcing some to dreadfully whiff the ominous burning white American cheese. But they may as well be if, that is, teachers like the explorer are not moving forward, and building leaders like Passenger 1B are not providing the professional development needed in order to grow current effective instructors.

Often, those who are living and breathing life into the unhatched eggs of our future are using some of the best practices in education, but they become complacent. There is no motivation, no drive, no leader pushing them to grow and self-reflect after delivering what they feel is good, solid instruction with subpar results. Students nowadays will read. They will research. They will write in argumentative, judgmental, and free-thinking form. But the vehicles for doing such are light years away from where they used to be, even as little as three to four years ago.

Wireless handheld devices have undoubtedly become the norm, as have social media outlets and opinionated talking heads on YouTube.

Those are their tools. Students certainly aren't using microfiche and burning the midnight lamp at the library anymore. Undoubtedly, teachers need to be literate users of the latest standard forms of communication to keep on par with their students.

Often, our building administrators aren't the ones with the skill set to drive the team forward in this mission through modeling, but more and more newer members of the profession *are* bringing these skills into the classroom. The next step is for the building leader to use these teacher leaders to bring these skills to the rest of the faculty.

All teachers must also be equipped with the latest understanding of recent developments in their practice, excluding "junk science," of course. They know or should know their discipline better than anyone outside their department in the same organization. For this, teachers need to read, research, borrow, create, and implement. Many strong leaders will take what they can from others with similar missions, adjust it so that it suits their needs, and recreate it, making it work. With that, one can harness the forgotten energy of the Romney Wordsworths and help breathe new life into them.

In order to avoid total obsoleteness, a good, strong educational leader must also foster effective professional development (PD) for all teachers in the building. There are two types of PD sessions that are common but perhaps worthy of scrutiny, just like that seven-legged dog that Sam the Breeder told you was "perfectly normal." The first one is the canned full-day "on-the-road" show. These sessions usually include an outsider taking center stage and a large audience taking notes, laughing at their jokes, and being given five minutes at the end to ask questions amid several rounds of applause.

They can be effective but often lead to a circus-like atmosphere tainted with people grading papers, figuring out how to pay their bills, or simply pretending to pay attention for as long as they can so that they're not called to the office later to explain how they're going to implement whatever it is in their classroom (next to the grilled cheese torture chair). Some of the better ones of this style tend to include periods of staff interaction and teacher-driven discussions on the topic on hand. Often, though, the audience is so diverse that they themselves have different goals in mind.

When this becomes the case, the effective school leader will group the audience according to goals and other common interests so that they may collaborate on the spot, extract targeted information, and then tailor that information to their needs. This will allow for meaningful feedback and professional development. It will also provide an administrator with clear parameters when checking for understanding and follow-through in the classroom.

The second style that may be effective, depending on how it is implemented, is the PD "smorgasbord." PD "smorgasbords" are normally whole-day or multiple-day conferences built around a common theme related to certain goals. This style is commonly found in national, regional, or state conferences and can be very effective. This is also an effective way to run professional development in one's building, providing that it has a central theme directly tied to the building's goals. These sessions genuinely tend to keep everyone's attention and muster up the most positive feedback, especially when in-house faculty are running some of the sessions. There are two essential elements to making any one of these a success:

1. The day or days built around a central theme: technology in the classroom, improving attendance, active engagement, differentiated instruction, constructivism, project-based learning. The theme must be directly tied to improved student outcomes and the building's or district's goals. A lack thereof will likely lead to a cool and interesting day but not much yielded in terms of measurable outcomes.

    It ends up being sort of like hitting the early-bird buffet. You scoop up a plateful of mermaid tail, and the next thing in line after the coffee is a bowl of brontosaurus eggs. There's no connection, and no one in their right mind would combine the two at the same setting.

2. Follow-through in the classroom. Far too often, knowledge gained through PD "smorgasbords," too, can fall through the cracks of Mars, only to lie idly for a million years to be rediscovered, unless there is some degree of implementation of something new in the classroom.

    An effective educational leader should employ the same basic strategies employed almost daily as a teacher. Check for understanding through observation, conferences, e-mails, and teachers' logs. Set aside the next PD day for teacher presentations or critical friend reviews. Without follow-up for the benefit of the child, there is no target.

The third type of professional development is one that we seldom see and possibly could bridge the gaps that develop between the Romney Wordsworths and school leaders of the world. And that is a complete and utter self-guided, teacher-driven, teacher-implemented practice, where teachers develop their own goals (directly aligned with the building's or district's goals), conduct their own research and trial and error, document their progress, and at some point present their findings to their immediate supervisor or team of teacher experts for feedback and assessment. Spin-offs of this style can often be included as an ongoing process in a school and can usually lead to stronger results. Again, without classroom follow-through, though, there is no point. There has got to be an impact on students.

The challenges here for the leader become management and time. Depending on the size of one's faculty, getting to each and every teacher on multiple occasions throughout the school year to determine how well they are progressing is difficult, to say the least, but it's not impossible. If this becomes the standard or even one of the standard practices for PD in one's organization, they must prioritize having small, meaningful meetings with teachers and a sharing of best practices. Or in a larger school, teachers ought to be trusted to work with one another and become critical friends while engaging in trial-and-error strategies and tracking their own data.

With such a practice embedded as a standard, the teachers can employ simple communication strategies to the leader or department head or anyone else who directly supervises them. This is clearly a less intimidating setting. Good leaders shouldn't be intimidating to begin with. Therefore, the only barrier truly is time.

Vital to the success of this style of professional development is the teacher's will and intrinsic drive to succeed. Crucial to guaranteeing that that happens is a fostering of a relationship similar to the friend-friend model in Confucianism. Teachers are the leaders of their classrooms, and an overarching dictatorship telling them that they are obsolete will only lead to doom like it did for the State's head in *The Twilight Zone*. Likewise, a leader who fails to address complacency, obsoleteness, or weaknesses when he or she sees it will also get subpar results from their teachers.

So for the passive, polite, and seemingly outdated "Passenger 1As" in your building, take the initiative to harness their strengths. Open up that time machine that they lost sight of somewhere along the way. Catch them being successful with new challenges, and have them take the lead on bridging their new ways with the same thing they did over and over again during the last seven hundred years.

Often, like Passenger 1A, they are some of our most well-liked classroom leaders and will effect change. To sweep them under the rug like the dust from the meteor that crashed into the master suite the other night will have a direct negative impact on students. Simply put, it's a surefire, five-minute cook time recipe for the building leader to become obsolete.

The Chancellor, or dictator, in "The Obsolete Man" could easily sweep every Romney Wordsworth under the carpet with the support of the council and members of their society. Yet, taking the opposite approach and keeping the Wordsworths around but not holding them accountable is just as counterproductive. Harness their best practices, attractive personalities, and seasoned reputations, and find ways to push them forward into the next millennium.

PASSENGER MANIFEST

1A
Name: The Explorer
Occupation: Teacher
Redeeming Qualities: Well-liked; knowledgeable about the Age of Exploration; creative; has the ability to build long-lasting positive relationships; strategies have led to long-term content retention
Atlantian Fields Usability Rating: 7/10
Leadership Potential: 5/10
Confidential Advisories: Trends toward mediocrity; does not use the most current practices with a vast majority of the curriculum he is responsible for; does not question authority; isolates himself from organizational matters.

1B
Name: The Explorer's Principal
Occupation: High School Principal
Redeeming Qualities: Has a good relationship with the Explorer; cares about results; works directly with some people who get sub-par results
Atlantian Fields Usability Rating: 5/10
Leadership Potential: 6/10
Confidential Advisories: Plays favorites, and everyone knows it; does not force change in a timely manner, if ever

1C
Name: Romney Wordsworth
Occupation: Librarian
Redeeming Qualities: Stands up to authority; will sacrifice his life and livelihood for the good of humankind and to force change
Atlantian Fields Usability Rating: 8/10
Leadership Potential: 8/10
Confidential Advisories: Did not develop with the times

1D
Name: The Chancellor
Occupation: Chancellor of Futuristic Dictatorial Society
Redeeming Qualities: None
Atlantian Fields Usability: 0/10
Leadership Potential: 0/10
Confidential Advisories: None

PLANNING FOR SUCCESS: KEY IDEAS

- One of the keys to successful leadership is to keep the professional team current through quality, targeted professional development. While there are several different known types of professional development practices in existence, rarely do educational leaders build programs that allow for teachers to focus solely on their current students. Without a leader who values both the art of sound teaching and academic growth, there exists a very real tendency for pockets of ineffective obsoleteness to develop.

- Once successful classroom strategies are realized, they should not only be celebrated but also shared in a constructive professional development setting with an open exchange between the successful presenter and the rest of the faculty.

PLANNING FOR SUCCESS: OTHER LEADERSHIP QUALITIES AND STRATEGIES

- One of the single most important traits that an educator can develop is the ability to foster lasting connections with their students, both past and present. This may be through a mild-mannered, passive demeanor; a superior knowledge of a particular concept; or simply a creative way of teaching a certain idea or course.
- A focus on student-centered activities creates a strong, solid teaching foundation, but results should reflect appropriate follow-through. Adequate assessments aligned with the standards must be used to determine the impact that any teaching style has on learning.
- When a teacher knows and enjoys a certain topic, their enthusiasm and/or creative method of delivery can be so contagious that the students pick up on it and learn it very well. However, when this is not the case for all topics, the imbalance of learning is evident in the teacher's results.
- Employing teaching strategies that most educators will agree are strong and sound is an adequate foundation for best teaching practices.
- When teachers become too complacent in teaching anything, their students will know it. Just as a teacher's enthusiasm could be contagious, their lack thereof could also be contagious.
- Teachers must focus on all individuals and employ more up-to-date resources.
- The art of teaching changes through time, and what worked in the past may or may not work with today's learners.
- There are a variety of needs in every classroom, and a one-size-fits-all strategy is as obsolete as an authoritarian leader.
- Knowing that there is a variety of engagement, follow-through, and reinforcement strategies, coupled with a huge array of learners

in most public schools, educational leaders need to keep their team current through prescriptive development. For instance, having AP teachers grasp the same "new" strategies as teachers of students who are years behind grade level will assuredly isolate one of those groups.
- If one size doesn't fit all in the classroom, then it should not fit all in the professional development setting.
- A leadership flaw is becoming complacent in the way that mediocrity is addressed. A hands-off method of ignoring a problem can be so contagious that the entire organization develops a mind-set of being just "good enough."
- When the leader of an organization does not value stronger results, growth, or professional development for all, mediocrity will be the umbrella that keeps the organization protected by anything that could positively affect its culture.
- When an interactive, meaningful relationship develops between the leader and their teachers as well as the professional developer and their audience, the team(s) will uncover strategies, concepts, mind-sets, and other relationships that they never before realized, embrace them, and move forward with improvement.
- No faculty member should be fearful of a leader, especially one with an imbalanced approach to working with team members.

REFLECTIONS FOR YOUR ORGANIZATION

- Are students retaining the knowledge and skills they are being taught? If so, are the skills and knowledge retained essential and serving a larger purpose?
- Do the organization's vehicles for delivery value the art of each teacher's skill set while also taking into consideration the variety of learners in the building—adults and students?
- Does the leader of the building desire culture over growth? If it is the former, then is that leader stifling progress by avoiding constructive feedback or eliminating any opposition to change?
- Does your building value the arts of teaching and learning?

NOTE

1. Rod Serling, *The Twilight Zone*, season 2, episode 29, "The Obsolete Man," aired June 2, 1961, on CBS.

Chapter 2

Build and Maintain Trust

If you are ever awoken in the middle the night by an unfamiliar humming sound somewhere in the distant sky and find yourself wandering to the back deck to catch a glimpse of history being made as we become the reluctant hosts of visitors from another galaxy, don't rush too quickly to make a judgment—either positive or negative. Rather, let your heart rate slow down to its normal pace, adjust your bifocals, make sure the liquor bottle's cap is screwed on tightly, and take a few deep breaths. Unfortunately, a rush to judgment could get you killed, abducted, or even brought before a new layer of a judicial system trying you for crimes against something that didn't exist prior to that historical night.

For avid *Twilight Zone* fans, season 3, episode 24's phrase "It's a cookbook" brings back haunting memories of a man—and much of a generation—who perhaps should have looked a proverbial gift horse in the mouth.[1] Without sticking a hand too deeply into the swirling vats of "To Serve Man," the protagonist of this classic, a sharply dressed, smooth-talking, somewhat savvy but naïve bureaucrat named Mr. Chambers, otherwise known as Passenger 2A on Flight 607, helps shape our next chapter.

Unlike Mr. Romney Wordsworth, Mr. Chambers is viewed by society as a fully functional and important member of modern America. In fact, he benevolently implies to some of his more militant colleagues that they may soon be obsolete based on the peace and prosperity that the futuristic voyagers have brought to our otherwise self-destructing planet.

Who are these voyagers? They are called Kanamits, of course, and the one Kanamit representing his species in New York City, where Mr. Chambers resides, is the antagonist of the story. He is also Passenger

2B. Simply put, the Kanamits strategically invade various parts of the globe and convince most earthlings that they mean no harm. But the story doesn't end there. In fact, that is only the beginning. Like Romney Wordsworth, Mr. Chambers, one could say, becomes the unfortunate victim of circumstance. He is simply the man who viewers follow as the new leaders of earth begin implementing positive changes far beyond anyone's wildest utopian imagination.

When the Kanamits landed on the streets of select cities worldwide, they did indeed come not combatively but rather quite peacefully. They were scrutinized at first but were eventually accepted by humans when they graciously eliminated hunger and ushered in peace and prosperity. It was only after a tenacious colleague of Mr. Chambers broke a code in a book accidentally left behind by the intergalaxy immigrants that their true motives were uncovered, and, it is found, they were not here to do what we thought, for there was an ulterior motive for wanting to keep earthlings alive and well, similar to keeping chickens, turkey, deer, and swine alive and well.

Generally speaking, most people are very trusting of those who are closest to them and complete strangers. Many may say that we don't trust the government, banks, or random passersby that we may glance at for a moment when shopping at the supermarket. In reality, however, the vast majority of Americans have a lot of trust in all of the above. There is trust in the safety of our local supermarkets and in the ability to meander through the aisles for as long as any customer would like without being accosted, mugged, harassed, or anything of the sort. There exists a trust that those simple painted lines on the roads are watching the moves of every motorist so that when people are out and about sightseeing, they can make it back home safely.

The concept of trust plays into the role of an educational leader every day with nearly every decision they make. For that reason, school administrators need to be truthful with their decisions. That is not to say that one shouldn't use the strengths of a program or certain faculty member to mask or override a weaker initiative. It is to say, however, that people who have ulterior motives that are uncovered never fully regain the trust of their colleagues.

It is important to note that being truthful does not mean showing all cards. Being truthful, in essence, means refraining from lying. Truth being told, one strategy in working with challenging parents, community members, or staff is to hold a proverbial "ace in the pocket." The ace in the pocket is simply like bringing a ray gun to a light-saber duel.

There is a real need to develop practices for working with every type of person, including those who are simply challenging and those who are irrational. Every leader has the potential to work with one on any given day. But neither a ray gun nor a plethora of ray guns can prevent school leaders from being sent into the freezing chambers of an early retirement. If ulterior motives to any major decision that one makes are exposed, it will be a long road to recovery.

Just ask Principal Deb Athlesford, Passenger 2C, and one of her favorite Global Studies teachers, Nanette Shortabred, Passenger 2D. Nanette makes history come to life, literally. During her middle school's annual mini-unit on the Viking invasions of Europe, the culminating activity takes place in the quaintness and security of Peaceful Hills, New Jersey.

Peaceful Hills is a sleepy little coastal town that took a small vacation when the great rush of newly freed slaves and European immigrants sought to start new lives in the industrial Northeast. It also took an uninterrupted nap when the GIs returning from World War II looked for affordable housing in America's suburbs. Most of the residents can lay ancestral claim to one of twenty or so founding "settlers" who started occupying the "rugged mountains" near the southern bay shortly before the turn of the century.

So, it is this town every year that Mrs. Shortabred chooses to have "sacked" by the overgrown, steroid-ridden savages from a forgotten century or two in world history. The townsfolk carefully plan for the Viking raids, and students, in turn, conduct interviews of the eyewitnesses and turn their newly found primary sources into a picture story. And speaking of forgotten history: In February 2019, the ever-reliable Mrs. Shortabred forgot to tell a substitute teacher how to close the lesson when she suddenly remembered that her daughter's wedding shower was the next day and had to leave abruptly to finalize plans.

The day went on like most days, and the substitute was highly effective in managing a rigorous series of forty-minute middle school study halls in place of the history lesson. The next day, the superintendent received a phone call from the mayor of Peaceful Hills. Knowing that Mrs. Shortabred did this every year, Mayor Greenfield always set up droves of bleachers for the townsfolk so that they could witness the annual pillage of the makeshift churches and homes strategically planted right on shore "for entertainment purposes only."

The police force always brought in backups from other jurisdictions, and all of its members gleefully reaped the benefits of a few overtime bucks on that particular day (speaking of Vikings). The problem that occurred that February was that Mrs. Shortabred never closed—or left plans to close—the lesson. After a fierce standoff with the men and women who swear to protect us—and most often do—and an order from the governor to deploy the New Jersey National Guard, the Vikings retreated to their boats and sailed back to Valhalla.

In summary, Mrs. Shortabred fell short of good judgment here. While no one was killed, maimed, or too psychologically distraught, the phone calls from the parents flowed like treasures being stolen from the wealthiest monasteries of Lindisfarne. The outcomes of one particular mistake were far reaching. Peaceful Hills soon set up an anti-Viking task force, later changed to the "Viking Management" task force due to some complaints from the politically correct town board watchers in the community.

Principal Athlesford was charged with writing a comprehensive board report on the matter. And a district-based team was developed for the sole purpose of creating a system of checks and balances for substitute teachers to ensure that they are informed on what to do with every child during each minute of the day.

Often, when events take an unexpected turn for the worse and there is a public outcry heard from the outer reaches of the Milky Way to the origins of the universe, a number of people react and look to overturn every unturned stone imaginable. At times, the focus is lost on the event itself or the person responsible for the matter to begin with. Additionally, a new system of micromanagement and impossibilities also develop.

Short of a brief interview with Principal Athlesford, Mrs. Shortabred seemed to escape the entire ordeal like a vampire's reflection in a house of mirrors. Rumors surfaced within weeks of the incident but soon died down, and things got back to normal. That is, until a group of angry parents got a hold of relevant and reliable information that suddenly turned everyone's attention back to that chilly February afternoon.

Mrs. Shortabred and Principal Athlesford, it turns out, had some rather compelling reasons to be a part of the solution rather than creators of the problem. It was soon revealed that Mrs. Shortabred's daughter's fiancé not only worked for the Peaceful Hills Police Department but also was the president of its union. Time and a half to ensure the town's tranquility and safety from the barbaric Norsemen came at a time when their failure to reach a new contract had put everyone's nerves on edge.

Athlesford didn't respond to allegations that there was some intentionality in "forgetting" to leave instructions for closing that lesson plan. Nor did she respond to the fact that her son was a majority owner in the T-shirt company that had annual exclusive rights to street vending during the event. By 2020, it was determined that the last annual Viking raid of Peaceful Hills, New Jersey, was itself going to sail into a frozen sunset forever. Although both Shortabred and Athlesford kept their jobs, they never fully recovered from what appeared to be a chain of mishaps that ironically worked to benefit people to whom they were related. Needless to say, it was assumed that both had ulterior motives for orchestrating the "mistakes" of that particular day.

This may seem like a far-fetched example, but many people inside and outside the world of education criticized the Common Core for a variety of reasons, some of which were related to communism and the ending of state's rights over their educational curricula. In 2013, New York State Commissioner John King ended a series of planned town meetings to promote the Common Core due to intense backlash from parents. Some who planned on listening to him and participating in a productive conversation suddenly found that such a conversation was not going to take place after all. Couple that with a plethora of statistics that one could find almost anywhere online about classified government space-age cover-ups, UFOs, extraterrestrial visitations to earth, and of course alien abductions, and it becomes clear that some may be thought to have ulterior motives when in fact they don't.

Educational leaders often find themselves in the spotlight, for both good and bad reasons. Regardless of which category your decisions slide you into, assume that at more points than not, you will find yourself on the defensive. Think before you act. Don't ever let perception cloud your judgment. Remember, administrators are not omnipotent. Providing answers without fully understanding those answers is not necessary. Making decisions without fully weighing all the impacts of one's decision is not advisable.

One thing is for certain, though: Don't bring change to the table if the decision for that particular change has already been made. Many schools have shared decision making as a codified core value or practice. When shared decision making becomes just a phrase for the organization, it's bad for morale. When it is an outright lie and cover for an administrator who wants to appear to be a leader, it'll draw more pitchforks out of the barn than Frankenstein's monster.

Unlike Principal Athlesford, Passenger 2E, Principal Stevens, employs strategies that strengthen and expand her teams. Stevens knows what she wants from her team members. After a series of constructive performance reviews by multiple direct supervisors, her strengths are clear. She is strong in prioritizing under pressure; clear in conveying her goals to her staff, supervisors, the board of education, and any parent who pays attention to the building's goals; even tempered when it comes to oppositional behaviors; and generally well liked and well respected in the building and community.

Stevens knows that her assistants bring other strengths to the table. Her long-time top assistant is fantastic with developing and managing schedules, interpreting contracts, and seeing ways to make seemingly impossible ideas work within the constraints of the school day. The newly hired assistant principal is a stickler for disciplining students while conveying to them that he is undeniably compassionate and traditional. Her other assistant principal is a master at constantly improving building security while maintaining a strong presence, being the most visible of the crew throughout the school day and at evening events.

But what Principal Stevens does best is tell people the truth. She is known to go toe to toe with superiors if she truly thinks that what they are bringing in is not totally in the best interests of students. She has been known to have uncomfortable but necessary conversations with soon-to-be exiting employees, people whose actions have negatively affected others, and her closest teammates.

When she doesn't know the answer to something or simply can't share the answer, she uses phrases like, "I can't answer that at this time," "I'll look into that," and, "Quite frankly, I don't know. That's a good question." She also tends to keep some of her cards close to her and safely guarded by her clenched fingers and remains quiet when opposing forces unite and are not working in her favor. Some of her most noteworthy catch phrases and pieces of advice that she's given throughout the years are:

- To kids in conflict: "Don't believe anything you hear and only half of what you see."
- To teachers at the opening-day faculty meeting: "Don't ever put your hands on kids, and don't use sarcasm with kids."
- To teachers she is evaluating: "What are they going to know or be able to do at the end of the class that they couldn't do at the beginning, and how are you going to know?"

For a moment now, it is appropriate to take a turn out of the world of science fiction and into reality and literally a life-changing moment. It was a typical cold January afternoon during the busiest open campus lunch period at a standard American high school. Approximately 700 students and staff were enjoying their only real "free" period of the day, while the leadership team was meeting with the RTI coordinator in the main office. In the middle of the discussion, a loud thud came from the center of the main office, and a maintenance worker was lying motionless on the floor. Two administrators responded and took a few seconds to assess the situation. Upon observing the worker's skin turn from its normal color to a pale blue, one administrator immediately hit the floor to give the worker two rescue breaths. He then looked at the other administrator and said, "Start your compressions."

The second administrator focused on his count—1 and 2 and 3 and 4 and . . . —at some point, realizing that the latest standards that he remembered did not call for rescue breaths. He then left the count and focused on pumping away at a firm and steady pace. While pumping, the second administrator looked up several times at one of the secretaries, asking if she had "called the codes." At one point, the secretary turned to the other secretary and asked what he had meant. That secretary calmly stated that a shelter in place had been called.

The administrator did not realize that it had been called and continued to focus on the chest compressions. He simply couldn't find the right words for "shelter in place," even though he had called dozens throughout his tenure. *One and two and one and two and one and two. . . .* The next one on the scene was the school nurse, hunched over the nearly lifeless body of the maintenance worker with scissors in hand, cutting the custodian's shirt off. The only thing that she said to the administrator doing the compressions was, "Keep going. You're doing well." By the time paramedics had arrived, a shock had been administered, and the maintenance worker's life had been saved.

The team's attention to quick action and working together as a natural response were the reasons. That natural response was borne of trust. Trust was the key to all of this. The first administrator trusted his instinct; the second trusted his partner and his secretaries. The nurse trusted her training and the administrator's method of pumping. From the utterance of the words "Start your compressions" to the secretaries calling a shelter-in-place to those who were left supervising students and to the athletic trainer who taught the administrators CPR and first aid, it was a trusted team effort, with no one working against the group.

Athlesford and Shortabred, on the other hand, were both caught manipulating a system so that it worked to their advantage. The Kanamit did the same thing. The difference here is that the Kanamit didn't work for a school. He worked for himself. In case you haven't figured it out by now (spoiler alert), the human race is gratefully served by the Kanamits, and in turn, those unlucky enough to board one of their flights back home simply to "explore" find themselves "served" to other Kanamits. Yes, Mr. Chambers—and the rest of us, I'm sure—make fine high-protein delectable treats for some cross-universe species searching the Milky Way's countryside for a source of food. When Athlesford and Shortabred's underlying motives were put out there for others to scrutinize, there was no turning back the clock.

So, if one night you ponder all of this while reveling in the breathtaking view of the thousands of visible stars twinkling overhead millions of miles away, take note of who else may be out there, hopping from one celestial orb to the other in some machine that defies all our known scientific laws. All of it may seem like an impossibility, that is, until one person, then another, then another start connecting those bright white lights in the sky, and before you know it, you're preparing for a ride with the Valkyries, and one of those planet surfers is prepping for the next leader to take your place.

Having ulterior motives and using a team or initiative to mask one's true motives can not only hinder progress and send one to a snack bar far away, but also break apart a team or prevent those natural teams from forming in the first place.

PASSENGER MANIFEST

2A

Name: Mr. Chambers

Occupation: US federal government intelligence agent

Redeeming Qualities: Strong small-team leader; fosters a sense of loyalty; his team will continue to work to meet their goal even in his absence

Atlantian Fields Usability Rating: 8/10

Leadership Potential: 7/10

Confidential Advisories: Jumped too soon to befriend an unknown enemy and thus let his guard down

2B

Name: Kanamit

Occupation: Alien ambassador to earth

Redeeming Qualities: Extremely knowledgeable in growing and producing foods

Atlantian Fields Usability Rating: 2/10

Leadership Potential: 1/10

Confidential Advisories: Very conniving and deceitful; self-serving; has been known to have ulterior motives

2C

Name: Deb Athelsford

Occupation: Middle school principal

Redeeming Qualities: Has a good relationship with at least one teacher who has a very strong method of delivery

Atlantian Fields Usability Rating: 1/10

Leadership Potential: 2/10

Confidential Advisories: Will conveniently slip under the radar when things go bad; has been known to have ulterior motives; made decisions that drastically changed an annual tradition; put the extended learning community at risk

2D

Name: Nanette Shortabred

Occupation: History teacher

Redeeming Qualities: Makes history come to life; creates hands-on learning; employs reading, writing, problem-solving, and project-based learning in her plans

Atlantian Fields Usability Rating: 5/10
Leadership Potential: 3/10
Confidential Advisories: Will conveniently slip under the radar when things go bad; has been known to have ulterior motives; made decisions that drastically changed an annual tradition; put the extended learning community at risk

2E
Name: Stevens
Occupation: Principal
Redeeming Qualities: Owns mistakes; is honest, truthful, trustworthy, and transparent; prioritizes; strong under pressure; instills leadership qualities in others; recognizes strengths of team members; understands that she is a part of a leadership team instead of a lone leader directing all underneath her
Atlantian Fields Usability Rating: 9/10
Leadership Potential: 9/10
Confidential Advisories: None

PLANNING FOR SUCCESS: KEY IDEAS

- Sound educational leaders must live and exemplify trustworthiness, transparency, and the ability to be prescriptive when making decisions. When a firm and lasting trust has been established, the team will bond so much that the natural flow of work and progress will permeate the organization.

PLANNING FOR SUCCESS: OTHER LEADERSHIP QUALITIES AND STRATEGIES

- Being trustworthy is a personality trait that is essential to any leader's success and potential.
- Those who have earned the trust of complete strangers they supervise will always have the support of those same people when forming teams, asking for assistance, and ensuring that operable systems are in place.

- Never should trust be equated to a total lack of issues or "problems" that need to be addressed by a school leader or their superiors.
- When those involved in any surfacing issue that calls for immediate investigation, review, and change know that their trustworthy leader is included, they will come to that leader's support, and the outcome of such an endeavor will lead to progress.
- Often, when something goes awry, school leaders should not only be ready to lead or be the subject of an investigation but also know that the teams and people involved are automatically put in a reactionary mode. Undoubtedly, by taking a few extra proactive steps, such issues could have been avoided altogether. Hence, the necessity of truthfulness in the organization.
- Daily, weekly, monthly, and annually completed tasks also require a system of trust and a trusted team. These tasks are those that school administrators are all too familiar with: disciplining students, hiring team members, budgeting, overall management of the building or district, program review and implementation, and professional development.
- The proactive, trustworthy leader will follow protocols when it comes to everything they do, especially student's legal rights. For instance, a student suspension may call for parental contact within twenty-four hours, a written reason for the suspension, and of course due process. A proactive, trustworthy leader will be very direct with the reason for the suspension; have the necessary conversation with the child's parent or guardian to finalize the suspension as a standard; and provide written notification immediately, even if they have a courier hand the guardian the document.
- Often, parents will want to make sure that what is happening to their child is fair and if others have been or are being treated similarly. The trustworthy leader will never speak about another child but will openly and honestly speak in generic terms about school practices and policies.
- When a leader reinforces their decisions through open dialogue, a system of trust develops.
- Knowing that every major decision made will have tentative or long-lasting consequences should by nature compel every school leader to be as open and honest with their decisions as reasonably expected.

- Truth and transparency should prevail not only when working with students and their families but also when working with anything that calls for an overhaul of existing programs or systems.
- If the building or district uses shared decision making when hiring employees, starting a new initiative, or simply changing the master schedule, then that process needs to be honored at all times.
- When there is pressure to stray from an agreed-upon process and simply make decisions because of other compelling forces that *could* have ulterior motives, honor the process and be truthful to those compelling forces.
- Abandoning the shared decision-making process and creating a situation in which a leader's supporters suddenly do not matter will lead to a breakdown in the process as well as a new notion that perhaps the leader is not as trustworthy as was previously thought.

REFLECTIONS FOR YOUR ORGANIZATION

- Who are the most trustworthy members of your immediate and more global teams? Why do you consider them trustworthy?
- What underlying motives or culturally identifiable intricacies informally permeate decision making? Do those same building or district attributes stifle progress and/or lead to a quietly imbalanced organization?
- When systems break down, who is responsible, and how do they react?
- Does a lack of trust in your organization hinder the development of effective teaming?

NOTE

1. Rod Serling, *The Twilight Zone*, season 3, episode 24, "To Serve Man," aired March 2, 1962, on CBS.

Chapter 3

Build Community

Maple Street, Fill-in-the-Blank, USA. An otherwise peaceful late summer afternoon was interrupted by a few minor disturbances. Everyone in the neighborhood was going about their usual business, when suddenly, the tools, amenities, and culturally changing inventions-turned-objects taken for granted ceased to function normally. Unbeknownst to the residents of Maple Street and the surrounding city blocks, an invasion had just taken place. It wasn't visible to the naked eye, nor did it come with beaming lights, roaring tanks, or screaming fighter jets. It came alright. But it came unnoticed. And there was no need for it to be disguised.

Who were these invaders in "The Monsters Are Due on Maple Street"?[1] Therein lies the tale. It's 1960. This is episode 22. Serling has just forced us to take a moment (or several) and stare into the mirror—not out of vanity but for reasons only most of us come to realize at some pivotal time in our lives. There is an inherent assumption in today's society that on any given day, one will have access to their computer, phone, microwave, refrigerator, car, or any means of transportation. And their self-control. But, if they woke up from a midday's nap and found that none of these things worked, they might chalk it up to a problem with the furnace or the local gas and electric company.

Taking this concept of not having the "essential" items that we take for granted a step further, one walks out onto their front porch. They are blindsided! They're not the only one experiencing inexplicable problems with their electronics. At first, everyone does the neighborly thing: tries to help each other out and look for logical solutions underneath hoods of cars and in basement power breakers. Then, when one or two people bring up the equally inexplicable unidentified flying object that flew overhead hours before, things turn ugly. The finger pointing on who knew what and how and when brings everyone's inner beasts out and into full-swing survival mode.

That is the premise behind "The Monsters Are Due on Maple Street." In classic Serling fashion, there exists a shift in gears, from ghosts and goblins, autocratic societies, and the vast darkness of doom and death to the lurking shadows of the human being's inner psyche and the enemy within. It's also the premise behind any community that seems to have everything it wants and needs and is suddenly, without remorse, thrown into the churner by circumstances beyond its control. In fiscally unstable times, such a situation can ruin a community and its principal school leader. Therefore, it is vital for effective educational leaders to try everything in their power to keep all of the monsters at bay.

Passenger 3A is also on today's journey. Rather than someone who was a victim of the supernatural or a proverbial villainous leader, Passenger 3A is someone who had probably stayed at school after hours on the day that the monsters arrived and began covertly wreaking havoc on the quaint bedroom Maple Street community. Passenger 3A, it turns out, was the superintendent of the Tall Carnivorous Oaks School District, which encompassed Maple Street, Sycamore Drive, Shrubbery Lane, and all the other idyllic roads in town.

Those who have been in the school business for fifteen to twenty years or more may remember the days of one-thousand-dollar classroom supply lines, annual field trips, and relatively low health care costs. Those days are gone—for now. Most people can adjust rather easily to a more restrictive supply order for next year's materials. Although they don't like it, they generally understand rising health care costs and contributions. But when it comes to significant changes in school personnel and their functions due to having to do more with less, there is potential for that friendly leprechaun—the one leading a faculty through Rainbow Fields to an empty pot of gold—to wind up in the front pages as a murder victim.

Perhaps an exaggeration. But knowing the history of almost any community plagued by a severe economic downturn, one could reasonably assume that labor unrest can be extremely violent. Not too long ago, most Americans had to struggle through the Great Recession. Certainly, a lot of them understood it and were perfectly content settling for less money or more work, especially when they worked for a school. Most people, maybe. But when a community's amenities are taken away or altered in some way, people generally have a "breaking point." Therefore, it is absolutely crucial to carefully craft change so that it directly affects every facet of a building or district.

Most people can live with the reality that "fair" isn't always equal. But very few can ever live with things being both unfair and unequal. Change can be very difficult, especially in places where everyone is used to fast times or a nice steady pace of living. Passenger 3A knows this all too well. When Tall Carnivorous Oaks underwent several rounds of changes in its economy, demographics, pride, and outlook for the future, its leader was naturally called upon to be "fiscally prudent" and continue to lead a system that outperformed other school districts with similar hindrances.

Passenger 3A wasted no time springing into action and preparing for the next budget season. The first order of business was to ensure that there weren't disproportionate blows to any one level of education or any one building. A meeting with the district's fiscal managers—principals, assistant superintendents, budgetary directors, and anyone else who was responsible for a budget—took place for two purposes: to share the goals (with hard-to-swallow facts and numbers) and to brainstorm ideas on how to do more or maintain the status quo with less money.

The wheels were in motion. Including all the fiscal managers not only generated an abundance of ideas but also allowed some to see what others were sacrificing for the good of the whole. In addition to that, those in charge of any segment of the overall budget began the process of cutting, whether it was paper for the copier, fresh water for the office employees, or a subscription to a seldom-used service by an outside agency.

Then came the third step: community involvement. Posting the state's woes and subsequent district quagmire on the web page is certainly acceptable but not nearly enough. Anyone who had a job that was lost or read the newspaper regularly or just simply turned the TV on knew how bad things were, knew that things were going to be cut. This is where real gains were made. Passenger 3A held community forums to solicit the public's input as well as give them the reality of the situation.

Each forum was held in a large space with plenty of seating, tables, parking, and accessibility. The sound system was checked and double-checked. Each board of education member had a microphone and copy of everything that was going to be presented well in advance, and the times and dates of the forums were posted and promoted.

Despite good intentions, it was here where the Tall Carnivorous Oaks monsters showed their fangs. People were accused of spending money in the past that shouldn't have been spent. Board members were asked how much of a pay cut they were taking, despite doing all of it for no pay at all. And every facet of the district, from the arts and athletics to the Astronomy Club and Aspiring Undertakers Society, seemed to have a representative who suddenly knew more about the history of their favorite and of course the most valuable program in the school district's history than anyone ever could have imagined.

However, for every five monsters who rolled up their fur and pounded their claws against the cafetorium's chair backs, there was a voice of reason—a voice similar to the very small minority on Maple Street who desperately tried to bring an opposing viewpoint to quell some who were more than anxious to chomp down on anyone in authority and grind them to an obliterated pulp.

As the forums continued and ideas—both good and bad—rolled in faster than conspiracy theories on Maple Street, small cuts were made easily. When it came to program cuts, Passenger 3A used all relevant data collected by her budget managers to determine which ones were unaffected, which ones were reduced, and which ones were eliminated entirely. Anytime an eliminated budget line affected a school, the school leaders were notified.

The real difficult cuts came with personnel. Here is where the true leaders had to carefully weigh their options against their goals and determine which personnel weren't "essential" when it came to accomplishing those measurable, widely publicized, agreed-upon, community-supported, student-centered goals. When all the possible "nonessential" employees were released, the next step was to excess some of those who were in a position to directly work toward accomplishing the goals but were unfortunate enough to be among the lowest in seniority or simply part of a program that could no longer be sustained.

But the key to the success of this process was the human touch that was put on it. Not only did Passenger 3A meet with each individual face to face to give them the unfortunate news, but she also had her key school leaders actively present during each uncomfortable and often tearful discussion. The final key to successfully taming the monsters of Tall Carnivorous Oaks was working with each bargaining unit on contract negotiations, ensuring that no one earned any raise that was clearly larger than the standard cost-of-living increase, especially the leader herself. Every team agreed to a small raise, either totally or nearly totally offset by an increase in health care contributions. This resonated with the community, while the program and material cuts resonated with everyone.

The fact that Passenger 3A became a victim herself greatly contributed to the notion that the community was a team, with not one member immune from the pestilence known as the Great Recession. In addition to backing up all cuts with relevant data, Passenger 3A set the stage for everyone who so desired to have a voice. She put together several meetings in advance of the larger meetings, which drew out the potential monsters. All the smaller meetings with school personnel and board members added up to a mutual feeling of everyone being in this together. The human touch on every employee who was cut provided not only nurture and comfort but also a clear message that there was hope that their job could be back when things turned around.

Finally, the physical setting that provided avenues for everyone to be involved also included a stage with the board members and superintendent Passenger 3A front and center of the team. Also present were those who supported the necessary cuts. Soon, the smaller, less fearful monsters of Tall Carnivorous Oaks took a chance and spoke in favor of the potential cuts that many others were opposed to.

As it turns out, superintendent Passenger 3A came out of the Great Recession with the same job, a minimal pay raise, fully supported by the board of education, and mostly supported by most residents of the district. Staying in her three-bedroom bungalow on Maple Street when the whole block turned on itself was a good decision. Taking the lead on managing a very sophisticated fiscal crisis and keeping the monsters of her district at bay was perhaps the best decision she had ever made.

In essence, when the leader of the pack makes cuts or decides to drastically challenge the status quo or implement changes that will assuredly have an impact on the culture of the organization, they must be sure that the ripple effects reverberate through every facet of the team. A freeze on salaries, for instance, should be a freeze on salaries for the leader as well as the followers. To pull a disappearing act when the shockwaves finally hit not only will be politically damaging but also will buy one a one-way ticket to a reserved space in a barrel of misfit administrators. Effective leaders will lead not only their immediate team members but also the whole learning community through challenging times.

PASSENGER MANIFEST

3A
Name: Unknown
Occupation: Superintendent of Tall Carnivorous Oaks School District
Redeeming Qualities: Builds community; plans; prepares; prioritizes; empowers team; builds teams; provides systems for nurturing and assisting those in need; treats all in the community equally; creates systems for allowing all to have voice
Atlantian Fields Usability Rating: 10/10
Leadership Potential: 10/10
Confidential Advisories: None

PLANNING FOR SUCCESS: KEY IDEA

- One of the keys to success in carrying through with the targeted mission of educating children when fiscal or other restraints tentatively hinder progress is to lead all teams and navigate the known and unknown challenges as a united community.

PLANNING FOR SUCCESS: OTHER LEADERSHIP QUALITIES AND STRATEGIES

- When a school or district is recognized for something celebratory and noteworthy, the leader will often be included in or the promoter of such a celebration. That same leader will take center stage when their building, district, or community is in crisis and lead them out of it.

- Very few people can accurately predict catastrophic or near catastrophic events. Effective leaders, however, can minimize the human tole that such events take on their community through a series of steps that keep the community together rather than tear it apart.
- Some events call for immediate action. When unforeseen circumstances turn to a call for action, bring teams together first. Next, empower each one. This not only builds trust and confidence but also allows every leader to be a part of the solution.
- Beyond the leadership teams, effective leaders provide forums and develop new systems that allow for an open exchange of information. Meaningful communication of all known facts needs to be realized by an entire community when it finds itself in a time of need.
- When effective communication and a careful analysis of assets and potential losses is brought to a community in need, an effective leader can change the view of the situation as well as the potential responses from the community members.
- An effective, transparent team-building leader will facilitate an entire community becoming a team, even when some members don't support all the decisions.
- Some will speak up and take a stand in favor of or opposed to the decisions affecting every facet of a building or district in need. However, eliminating the inhuman assets while providing a nurturing and supportive human touch to the people being lost through attrition will lead to more support for the school leader through challenging times.

REFLECTIONS FOR YOUR ORGANIZATION

- Are funds being adequately allocated at the present time?
- What plans exist for appropriately addressing a fiscal crisis?
- Who are the key budget managers in the organization, and how well do others know their budgets?
- How do the leadership teams embrace opposing views from those inside the organization and in the community? Do the teams

validate, consider the opinions of, and empathize with others who may disagree with them?
- In what ways are you building your community?

NOTE

1. Rod Serling, *The Twilight Zone*, season 1, episode 22, "The Monsters Are Due on Maple Street," aired March 4, 1960, on CBS.

Chapter 4

Think outside the Box

Imagine waking up one day in a room. It's dark enough to scare you, but a trickle of natural light allows you to determine that some nearby silhouettes are actually other people in the room with you. You don't have any idea where you are, why you are there, or even who you really are. It soon becomes clear that there are five in all: a ballerina, an army major, a clown, a bagpiper, and a hobo, all easily identifiable by their clothing.

The major has been plucked from that room and brought along on Flight 607's journey, right in seat 4A. If you've ever seen the *Twilight Zone* episode "Five Characters in Search of an Exit," you'd know why.[1] The premise just described is precisely what happens to the main character in this unique classic.

As is the case with other Serling masterpieces, the story starts off leaving the viewer intrigued by the simple yet mysterious opening scene. The major wakes up, not knowing where he is or how he got there, and quickly meets the others, who are in the same unfortunate predicament. Panicked, he searches all the walls of what appears to be a cylindrical cell for an exit of some sort, only to be chided by the rest, convincing him that he is wasting his time and energy. They explain they, too, had run their hands and feet by every square inch of the wall and floor with no success.

The one glimmer of hope they have is that every now and then, an entrance some thirty-five to forty feet above them seems to open. This isn't encouraging enough, however, as none of them has any tools to reach the top of the walls. They try using their hands and simple possessions, such as the clown's umbrella, to pound through the wall or dig into the floor but this, too, proves to be ineffective, for the whole wall is made of metal.

After his pleas to drive the team forward and continue trying fall on closed, defeated minds—as does his attempt to stab through the wall with his own sword, which breaks—the major listens to the clown bellow out a sarcastic one-liner about scaling the wall. The ballerina isn't humored. Rather, she's motivated by his joke and suggests that they try it. The idea is quickly shot down because of the lack of tools—that is, until the major develops a plan for them to stand on each other's shoulders and have the ballerina climb to the top to at least see what's out there.

The plan almost works, diverted by the unbearably loud ringing of what sounds like a church bell. As soon as the ballerina reaches for the top after climbing the four-man ladder, the bell shakes the team's stability, and they all come crashing to the floor like ten pounds of toys in a nine-pound torn Santa Claus bag. After their first attempt fails and the ballerina suffers an obvious but not serious injury, the major, with his tenacity and leadership skills, takes over.

First, he convinces the group that being close is worthy of another try. He then develops a new plan that doesn't include the ballerina. The team would use what remains of his sword along with the four-man ladder. Rather than being on the bottom, he would connect his sword to a rope, climb to the top of the ladder, and use the new tool as a hook. The team frowns upon the idea, primarily because they don't have a rope. At that point, the major quickly improvises, telling them all that they could easily use strips of their clothing. Within minutes, the plan works.

While most thought he was crazy to even consider trying to get out of their predicament and just accepting the status quo, the major took the lead with encouragement, logic, a little bit of wisdom, and a lot of creativity. That is why the major is on this journey as Passenger 4A. The major doesn't work in an educational setting. Yet his drive to succeed and think outside the box is precisely what every team needs in at least one of its leaders. This same mind-set could and should be employed when dealing with any number of issues that plagues any educational institution on any given day of the year.

Take the following standard so-called barriers that educators regularly face from time to time:

- a high school senior who is looking to take more advanced courses than her schedule allows
- a middle school student who doesn't exhibit any behavior problems yet hasn't passed a core class in two years and has no learning disabilities
- an elementary child who comes into the third grade without the ability to read

There are traditional approaches to resolving all these. There is also a plethora of nontraditional approaches that one could employ in order to produce a win-win outcome. Not every solution has to end in something being sacrificed in exchange for a gain. In fact, a strong team will have more win-win options on the table for such sticky scenarios than win-lose solutions.

A win-win approach starts with the leadership team and takes years to become an embedded practice throughout the school. While some will undoubtedly always think outside the box, their solutions may not always be the most advantageous to all involved parties. This is why it is crucial for the leader(s) to not only include several others in the process of troubleshooting but also have them take on the lead role when they've proven totally capable of doing so.

For the previous scenarios, the following would truly benefit the leadership team and, of course, students:

- a guidance counselor or perhaps a dually certified teacher
- a social worker, psychologist, or parent of a not-so-traditional child
- a reading or AIS specialist teacher with experience in multiple levels of teaching or simply an adult who normally comes in early, leaves late, and actively participates on building committees

Strong leaders will develop unique solutions that haven't been thought of or tried in the past and use the school's existing parameters—professional and nonprofessional contracts, the bell schedule, the start and end times—to their advantage. Be a creator, and don't let *creation* be a synonym for *invention*. Don't let *inventor* be a synonym for *creator*. Inventors build machines and parts. Creators bring life.

Take the following scenarios as a short and simple yet creative guide to thinking outside the box:

- In New York State, each student is required to pass a math New York State–created Regents Examination. Student X is a senior who has passed every other exit exam except for math. In reviewing her transcript, she moved during her junior year and returned as a senior. Prior to that, she had struggled to pass algebra but did well in geometry. Her algebra exam score was in the 30s, and the required score for credit for the same exam is a 65. It is March. The exam is in late June. Every other student in the building who graduates passes the Algebra Regents Exam.

  After working together on a schedule that allows the student to graduate on time with all twenty-two units of credit, an administrator–guidance counselor duo decide to put her into an academic intervention class with a geometry teacher and sign her up for the both the Geometry and Algebra Regents Exams. June comes around, and Student X fails the algebra but passes the geometry exam. Cap and gown ordered!

- Student Y has been chronically absent during his senior year. He has passed all his required exit exams but risks on-time graduation due to perpetually skipping the classes he doesn't like. His assistant principal has worked various angles tirelessly, including but not limited to suspending him, having a phone and in-person conference with his father, working with the athletic director to have him sit for two baseball games, and being kind and nurturing.

  The onus falls on him, but he hasn't made any adjustments, and time is running out. An easy solution is to hold baseball over his head. Cut school, we cut baseball. Simply put, baseball is a privilege. The football coach gets wind of this student's woes and is quick to point out to the administrators that a team once tried that with a football player and lost him altogether.

  The assistant principal tries a different approach, one that is neither benevolent nor punitive. She writes a personalized letter to Student Y that outlines the following facts:
  - the graduation requirements
  - the number of classes missed
  - the steps taken by everyone else to remedy the situation
  - an invitation to speak with a counselor for emotional support
  - a suggestion to work with his guidance counselor to develop a schedule for a fifth year of high school based on the fact that

the district budgetary constraints (which he doesn't understand) may not allow for a summer school program this year

The assistant principal copies Student Y's father, and neither he nor his child was very happy about her approach. Two things that did happen though: He started to attend all classes and wasn't benched for baseball. At times, showing the true dismal consequences of one's actions can have far-reaching effects.

- Student Z has a packed schedule and is still going to fall short one credit. This is mainly due to her poor performance during her junior year, when she became involved in drugs, alcohol, missing school, and other delinquent behaviors. The one glimmer of hope that her alert guidance counselor uncovered was a failed science class by only five points during her freshman year. She never retook the class. Instead, she moved onto another science class and passed it easily.

  Rather than having her sign up for summer school or a fifth year of high school, the guidance counselor and director of guidance worked with the building administration to collapse a class, find other students slightly behind on credit, and offer an in-school credit-recovery class during lunchtime. The student now has a choice: eat lunch while working on improving one marking period from that class from that particular year or staying in high school for an additional summer, semester, or school year.

- Student XYZ is an angry young man with an angry father. No one is immune to a childish outburst from time to time. However, generally speaking, public embarrassment isn't a normal occurrence in most settings. Those seasoned in public education—whether it be in the classroom, the halls, the athletic turfs, or behind a desk—know all too well that there are plenty out there who will not hesitate to almost skillfully have an outburst in school for anything from not getting his or her way to something that they or their child did or didn't do.

  Mr. XYZ often uses intimidation to get his child out of this or that while his son causes more issues in the building than every member of the Drama Club combined on the auditorium's stage. Most school personnel bend to Mr. XYZ because he's a "squeaky wheel," and they often find it difficult to "prove" that his son did this or that, knowing that it's always his word against someone else's. Dean Copper knows that neither Mr. XYZ nor his son plays by the rules, so to speak, so he does the same thing.

Rather than going toe to toe with Mr. XYZ, he embraces him, makes him a part of the solution rather than the problem. His standard lines to Mr. XYZ include:
- Here is what happened.
- I'd like your assistance with . . .
- How can we work together to . . . ?
- What is your ultimate goal for XYZ?

What Dean Copper realizes that no one else does is that Mr. XYZ really lacks control in his life and finds any way possible to gain it through his son's rather deplorable behavior. So Copper uses that to his advantage, and rather than sharing his authority and knowledge with Mr. XYZ, he lets Mr. XYZ partner with him as a friend-friend in Confucianism to essentially get what he, Dean Copper, wants anyway.

When dealing with angry people, becoming elevated often lessens every form of control that was present beforehand. Heightening an adversarial employee, parent, or student can only escalate a situation from bad to DEFCON 2. No one should have as their landing zone a cold, cylindrical metal cell adorned with plain walls and littered with other "misfits" (a hint to the twisted ending to "Five Characters in Search of an Exit"). Calm, cool, collected behavior will often lead to a reasonable conversation with a win-win solution.

No one is entirely immune to the natural response of fighting or flighting from an adverse situation, but when keeping the end in mind, one often finds that even the angriest of people can take it down several notches when they feel as though one is truly working in the best interests of their child. Effective leaders are professional and nonjudgmental. Taking a civilized yet "blue-collar" approach will land a quality team in the thank-you pages of the local internet sounding board rather in the middle of a chemical reactor meltdown.

Modeling such an approach for others will assuredly get the entire organization moving in the direction of effective conflict resolution. It won't happen overnight, but if it could change the way one child, one parent, and one staff member handles conflict, it'll spread and sooner or later become an embedded part of the school culture. This is especially crucial when it comes to leading a team. Principal Stevens won't make on-the-spot decisions if the potential ripple effects could land her in the metal cylinder. But she will communicate her thought process and ask nonjudgmental but pointed questions, usually to provoke others to think in the same frame of mind as well as to help her through her own thought process.

Thinking outside the box doesn't always have to equate to creativity. Thinking outside the box also means that one must develop a mind-set that yields second, third, and fourth steps; ripple effects; and the pros and cons of every decision made. Not every decision can be made in a split second. That is why it is crucial to know when and how to prioritize. Being a leader means that one will make important decisions every day. It could be as little as how to word a mass e-mail to parents, as big as where to harbor students and staff during an unexpected tornado, or as ironic as being in the bus lane to greet students when an errant passerby runs through the stop signal and nearly takes someone's life.

Think about each of those decisions as a book going into one's backpack. Every book is filled with pages of real and potential outcomes. Some of those books are light paperbacks, while others are thick, hard-covered encyclopedias. Every afternoon when the computer is shut down, all return phone calls are made, and the office doors are locked, that backpack is picked up and thrown over the shoulder. A second arm reaches back and slips through the second strap. That backpack is carried home every single day. It starts off light, but eventually, it gets heavier and heavier, until one day, it is very difficult to pick up.

PASSENGER MANIFEST

4A
Name: The Major
Occupation: Make-Believe Army Major
Redeeming Qualities: Creative thinker; motivates team members; optimistic; resourceful; develops and shares his vision
Atlantian Fields Usability Rating: 10/10
Leadership Potential: 10/10
Confidential Advisories: None

PLANNING FOR SUCCESS: KEY IDEA

- Creative thinkers will drive a team to succeed even under seemingly impossible circumstances. Effective educational leaders will not only think outside the box themselves but also encourage creative thinking and problem solving to permeate their organization through their team members.

PLANNING FOR SUCCESS: OTHER LEADERSHIP QUALITIES AND STRATEGIES

- Win-win solutions to problems that arise in any organization take time to develop.
- Embrace opposing forces when working together toward a common expectation.
- Effective leaders will use the existing tools that are at their disposal to overcome obstacles.
- Modeling effective conflict resolution will lead to better outcomes for an organization.
- Ask nonjudgmental questions when working with someone in an adversarial position.
- Know how and when to prioritize.

REFLECTIONS FOR YOUR ORGANIZATION

- How are solutions developed in your organization and by whom?
- Who are the informal leaders of your organization who develop outside-the-box solutions to everyday problems?
- Which obstacles pose challenges that the building or district never seems to overcome? What solutions have not been tried? Why haven't past attempts to ongoing problems been successful?

NOTE

1. Rod Serling, *The Twilight Zone*, season 3, episode 14, "Five Characters in Search of an Exit," aired December 22, 1961, on CBS.

Chapter 5

Be Empathetic and Compassionate

The phrase *walking on eggshells* should never be used, felt, acted upon, or entered into the culture of any fiscally sound organization. Nor should it be an underlying fear attached to any school district whose mission is to produce strong learners and productive, progressive thinkers. The moment one feels they need to keep their opinions to themselves so they aren't eliminated by their boss should be the same moment they sharpen their résumé and find a new job. The Machiavellian approach of ruling by fear is something that should have stayed where it originated: in a distant land and a distant time. When describing one's boss, a few adjectives should never be used: *mean, intimidating, cunning, conniving, sly, deceptive*. Each word, along with hundreds of others, has indeed been used by people in various organizations to describe a range of different bosses.

A leadership strength rarely highlighted in interviews or literature is being *well-liked*. Ultimately, everyone in education is working with or for learners. To be *respected* but not *liked* isn't optimal. Being *intimidating* but *liked* is only good for some members of the organization. Being *active, proactive, reactive*, or any other *active* word is fine but not when paired with *not liked*.

When leaders are liked, they're often described as someone who has an "open door." Having an open-door approach doesn't necessarily mean that anyone can come into one's office at any time to discuss whatever they want. It does, however, mean that a good, strong leader who is well-liked is also approachable.

Schools are just like most other institutions in our society: Safety enhances productivity. Simply put, children can't learn if they don't feel safe. Employees won't produce if they don't feel safe and supported. Just ask the residents of the small midwestern farming community that was the backdrop for the *Twilight Zone* episode "It's a Good Life."[1] Like the residents of Maple Street, the people of Peaksville, Ohio, had to live their lives with a monster—except this monster wasn't the kind who suddenly appeared out of nowhere and wreaked havoc on the community by taking away their amenities.

Oh, he took away their amenities, alright, but not for the reasons cited in "The Monsters Are Due on Maple Street." This monster took away everything that he simply didn't like, and he lived with the residents of his hometown forever. Similar to those whose fangs, claws, and spikes protruded from their bodies when the recession peaked in Tall Carnivorous Oaks, this monster was indeed a member of the school district who looked and acted just like any one of those monsters and those who spoke logically at the same meetings and the ones due on Maple Street. This monster didn't disguise himself behind pine trees and then come out at night to terrorize innocent bystanders. He didn't snatch wives, babies, or the residents' favorite pets from their backyards. No. He didn't need to stoop to those levels. He was just too sophisticated.

This monster's name: Anthony Fremont. One look at Anthony and one might reminisce about their own childhood. He could be seen jumping across his large front yard between the old oak trees or hopping over the chipped white-painted porch rails. His innocent looks and playful imagination would assuredly put a smile onto the faces of any passersby who took a wrong turn and mistakenly traversed the Ohio countryside searching to get back onto the main road.

But neither of those should fool anyone. Anthony, as it turns out, was no ordinary child. He had very special powers. Anything he didn't like, he didn't have to deal with. Worse yet, he could make it disappear. Whether it was a toy, animal, machine, other child, or any person who erroneously crossed him the wrong way, made a noise he didn't like, looked at him funny, or anything else, it could be wished into the cornfield across the street. From there, it never returned. To feel safe and secure in Peaksville, Ohio, where Anthony resided, was about as doable as convincing the devil that you'll gladly agree to sell your soul for fame and fortune but only with the added caveat of getting it back when you die. Anthony ruled by fear and intimidation and, as a result, controlled everything in town, from what everyone ate to what they watched on television.

Anthony has not boarded this flight. His leadership style is precisely the opposite of what is wanted in Atlantian Fields. Someone else, however, has come along. That someone is Passenger 5A, also known as Dan Hollis. Dan was once a resident of the same farming community that Anthony ruled over. Like many others from that town, he was once wished into the cornfield. It was there he resided until he was magically revived. After shaking off the dirt and clearing his mind, it was explained to him that he was now in good hands. Peaksville, Ohio, and its monster are long gone. They themselves are just about as alive as everything that found its way into the gravely cornfield.

Dan straps himself into his seat and prepares for the long journey ahead long before anyone else, for he, like everyone else, has a new lead on life. Prior to this, he lived under Anthony's reign of terror until one day, when he had consumed a little too much brandy. It happened to be his birthday, and he decided to test his fate with the six-year-old demon. Dan wanted to listen to one of the few remaining Perry Como records in town. Anthony, however, had other plans. In short, Dan lost. After being turned into a jack-in-the-box and placed in the corner of Anthony's living room, where everyone else gasped then turned away in horror, he was wished into the cornfield and disappeared on the spot.

Although he didn't live to truly end the monster's reign of terror, he was the only one in town with the courage to say something back to Anthony and try to get someone, anyone, to help end the torture. That is precisely why we picked him and gave him a first-class seat, along with several free shots of brandy. It is abundantly clear that Dan needs some help. Hopefully, he will get that help by sitting next to Passenger 5B, Ms. Helen Foley from the 1983 version of "It's a Good Life," which was a segment on Steven Spielberg's *Twilight Zone: The Movie*.[2]

Ms. Foley, schoolteacher, is named after one of Mr. Serling's high school English teachers at Central High School in Binghamton, New York. In this version of the story, she has the unfortunate experience of having backed her car into Anthony while stopping for a break in a nearly deserted, one-traffic-light town. She gives him a ride home and soon becomes a witness to the horrors that Anthony has unleashed on anyone who has tried to distance themselves from him or simply has something less than nice to say about him or his wishes.

But prior to feeling the impact of Anthony's reign of terror, Ms. Foley actually connects with him. While he transports one of his sisters into a cartoon wrought with a demonic butcher and other creatures from the pits of Hell chasing her and magically gives life to similar evil creatures in the living room, Ms. Foley watches in sheer terror, just like every other prisoner in the house.

What Ms. Foley does next, though, is the turning point in the episode and the reason she has been brought along as a Passenger 5B. She turns to Anthony and demands that he wish the demons away. She tells him firmly and without hesitation. She doesn't yell or scream or make any threatening movements toward him. She looks at him rather than the demons and firmly tells him until he listens. Ms. Helen Foley, at that moment, doesn't let Anthony see her fear.

What happens next is a reverse in magic brought about from Ms. Foley's natural ability to understand, nurture, and work with children—all children. Anthony wishes everything away. In the last scene, he is with her only. They appear to be in a thick fog with no one else around. When she asks him where he sent them, he replies that he sent them away from him, where they all wanted to be. Despite appearing to be an evil child with abilities far beyond the craziest of nightmares, Anthony has internalized not only the fear that everyone had around him but also the feeling of abandonment that came about first with his parents, as he mentions to her.

Helen Foley, whether through instinct, practice, or simple survival, follows up with a conversation on working together to help one another overcome what he can manipulate with his wishes and a kind but clear warning that he, in essence, needs to be careful what he wishes for, for it doesn't always work out to make him feel any better. Finally, she tells Anthony that she will not leave him and will indeed be with him from that moment on.

Most adults have come across a spoiled child at some point in their lives. None can successfully wish anything it doesn't like into a cornfield. There are, however, teachers, administrators, and others in our school buildings who can do something similar on a lower scale with anyone who doesn't agree with them. They are well known. They can be seen in the mail rooms, on the football fields, in the staff lounges, and in the classrooms. They may be known to have led multimillion-dollar or billion-dollar corporations or even schools and school districts. They lurk with familiar faces, everyday hairstyles, and traditional attire.

They are married and single; drive trucks, sedans, sports cars, or motorcycles; and do laundry, dishes, dinner parties, and everything else that many others do. But after getting to know them, one will eventually conclude that there is something missing. When that something is compassion and human empathy, the missing pieces of the puzzle suddenly come together to form a very clear picture of who they really are.

As educators, they are somewhat careful to disguise their true selves. They can get away with that so long as they don't break the law. Some do end up breaking the law, and it is only then when they are forced to resign. Knowing who they are and what their modus operandi is, is only half of the battle. In fact, it's the easy half. Calling them out and making them obsolete (for good reason) is the challenging half.

No one, however, can do this single-handedly. Dan Hollis is bold enough or rather drunk enough to make a desperate attempt to get someone to literally kill Anthony. He fails for a number of reasons. First, he responds to a situation with violence and no self-control. If history has taught nothing else, leaders who rule through violence and no self-control never survive. Similarly, educational leaders who "rule" through intimidation and fear also don't survive. Dan Hollis also acts out of desperation with only one thing in mind: survival. He has no plan, no shared vision, and everyone in town, despite living in constant fear, is surviving and getting by.

The single most important reason Dan fails is because he isn't a leader. Dan hasn't done his homework. He garners no support from anyone in town, and most people there probably knew he was going to explode when he did and just sat still for fear that they would be the next victim. Putting a quality team in place to develop a thorough plan usually starts with an idea and a small group before growing larger and gaining traction.

Certainly, Dan likely isn't in a position to actually plan Anthony's demise but perhaps he could have been. Anthony has the ability to make his evil wishes come true. But as we learn through Ms. Helen Foley, he also has the desire for human companionship and a need to feel included. She uses this not only to her advantage but also to actually partner with Anthony and at the same time lead him to a much better place.

When in a position of authority in a school, one who lacks compassion needs to be called out and removed as soon as possible. Compassion is a character trait that must be a part of the biological makeup of a true school leader. Those who aren't truly compassionate can mask their lack of compassion, but they will eventually be known. Like the specter that's been reported scaling the walls at Glenwood Cemetery, people will see right through them but also run like hell to avoid them. Usually, it's for good reason: They like keeping their jobs.

Getting rid of fear mongering is something that is essential to the health and safety of any well-functioning school. Not doing so would leave every employee checking their every move for fear that someone is watching and waiting for that moment to tell them, "Gotcha!" It breeds inefficiency, hesitation to take risks, and a sense of isolation and fear. The strategies and vehicles for ridding an organization of fear mongering differ based on who the monsters are. In the case of Anthony Fremont and other children, the abilities to empathize and nurture will allow teachers and educational leaders to partner with children and help them grow.

Their brains are still developing, and there is so much to be gained from teaming with them to provide them with all the necessary skills to become a better person. A strong emphasis on the need to expand the interactions between those students and school social workers is a must, as are the appropriate connections between all adults in the building and those particular children.

With regards to fear-mongering adults, effective school leaders simply need to employ every strategy possible to rid their school of them. This begins with documentation of incidents, up-front and honest conversations, and a detailed paper trail. A failure to do so will negatively affect not only the other teachers in the building but the leadership team, as well.

When the person in authority lacks the essential qualities of human nurturing, even on the slightest scale, there is no feeling of family or community. Teachers will do their jobs because it is their job. They'll follow the rules, do extra work for extra pay, and keep to themselves or the small clique of colleagues who have earned their trust. What they won't do is go the extra mile for someone whom they despise.

When the time is right, they'll finally land a position in another school or district ripe with spirit, pride, and togetherness, crucial components of an effective team. Any team that can arguably boast such traits will undoubtedly have the foundation to move forward through any obstacle with confidence. Any team that can't is simply not a team.

PASSENGER MANIFEST

5A
Name: Dan Hollis
Occupation: Unknown
Redeemable Qualities: Courage
Atlantian Fields Usability Rating: 1/10
Leadership Potential: 1/10
Confidential Advisories: Acts on instinct; uses violence to get what he wants; does not develop a plan; very little effort to gather support for a common cause

5B
Name: Helen Foley
Occupation: Schoolteacher
Redeemable Qualities: Firm; direct; nurturing; compassionate; embraces all children; knows when to act; bold enough to not allow for scare tactics to dissuade or intimidate her; speaks honestly; partners with children
Atlantian Fields Usability Rating: 10/10
Leadership Potential: 10/10
Confidential Advisories: None

PLANNING FOR SUCCESS: KEY IDEAS

- Effective school leaders will lead with compassion and empathy rather than through fear and tyranny. While demonstrating these traits through their work with students, teachers, and parents, they must also eliminate those in their organization who are discontent and lack the same qualities.

- When working with children who appear to lack the same standards of human empathy, it is crucial that school leaders and their teachers partner with students, build necessary connections, provide targeted social and emotional support, and use all the inside and outside agencies as much as possible to prevent them from becoming unstable adults.

PLANNING FOR SUCCESS: OTHER LEADERSHIP QUALITIES AND STRATEGIES

- Safety is an essential ingredient of both progress and learning. Children cannot learn if they do not feel safe in their environment. Teachers and other school employees will not grow if they do not feel the same sense of safety under their leader.
- Educators and support staff who interact with children need to be compassionate and empathetic to their needs.
- Embrace all children unconditionally. Students come from such a variety of backgrounds that educators must do what they can prescriptively to address their needs. However, one common practice and enduring belief that will envelop a strong, successful organization is that acceptance of all, regardless of how those children have traditionally responded to adversity.
- Quality leaders will have a nurturing effect on the children and adults in their organization through compassion and empathy. That ability to provide a nurturing environment will lead to voice, an open and progressive atmosphere, and an abundance of ideas.
- Fear mongering must be eliminated altogether in a productive, collaborative environment.
- Feeling included and connected are basic human needs. Fostering an educational environment where the students, teachers, parents, and others value these will open up broad pathways for educational leaders.
- High-quality educational leaders will value and be open to the ideas and opinions of others. They will embrace diversity in thinking, and others in the organization will do the same. So long as the team's goals are for the educational well-being of all children,

all in the organization will feel safe in sharing their opinions and ideas.

REFLECTIONS FOR YOUR ORGANIZATION

- Does your school or school district value the educational opinions of those in the organization—teachers and administrators?
- Are all children in the organization fully embraced and connected with an adult?
- How does the organization address the needs of students and guardians who are together isolated from the educational process?
- What systems are in place for ridding the organization of fear mongering or preventing it from occurring?
- Are counseling memorandums and other measures taken by school leaders to minimize and/or eliminate fear mongering direct, detailed, and effective?

NOTES

1. Rod Serling, *The Twilight Zone*, season 3, episode 8, "It's a Good Life," aired November 3, 1961, on CBS.

2. Joe Dante, John Landis, George Miller, and Steven Spielberg, dirs., *Twilight Zone: The Movie* (Burbank, CA: Warner Brothers, 1983).

Chapter 6

Believe in the Magic of Every Child Every Day

The year is 1847. Chris Horn is one of the brave American pioneers who may not be included in any of our history books but took the same chance as thousands of others traversing the countryside to reach what many considered a more promising land: California. Like other wagon trains, Chris's team encountered extreme conditions. Some felt the extreme cold of the Sierra Nevada Mountains, while others fought off hostile Native American tribes looking to protect their land and way of life. Chris Horn's team trekked through the extreme heat of the American Southwest but took a detour into *The Twilight Zone*. This is season 2, episode 23, "A Hundred Yards over the Rim."[1] Chris Horn is also on this flight, slipping through time again as Passenger 6A.

While short on supplies, including medicines, water, and food, the team is faced with a desperate situation. Pessimism takes over, and Chris's wife suggests that he search for a shaded spot to bury their infant son, now on the eleventh day of an unsuccessful battle against an unknown sickness. Chris won't hear anything of a burial and tells his wife and another pioneer that he is going to head over a "rim" to see if he can find a source of water and some game to hunt.

When Chris traverses a mountain of sand, he finds himself suddenly in New Mexico in 1961. After nearly getting run over by a truck and accidentally grazing his arm with a round from his own rifle, Chris stumbles on a roadside diner owned by a couple who offers him some assistance. They contact the local doctor, thinking that Chris is delusional and needs medical attention. As he is in the back room of the diner resting, the doctor evaluates him and finds him to be "normal," other than having delusions of being an 1840s traveler.

Among other modern inventions and developments, Chris is introduced to penicillin and stumbles across an encyclopedia that he sifts through. He soon comes across the name of his own sick child, who died in 1914 after a successful career in pediatric medicine. Chris is bound and determined to get back to his wagon train to move his team forward and save his child. He grabs his rifle and the bottle of penicillin and runs back toward the rim.

To the café owner and doctor, he disappears into the sand. To those waiting for him back in 1847, he appears, after only being gone for a few minutes, with penicillin and a new outlook to lead the others to their destination and into the future. He directs his wife to administer two penicillin pills to their sick son and tells another pioneer, Charlie, that there is a lot more over that rim, knowing that he just stepped into the future more than one hundred years.

The lessons learned from this episode are absolutely crucial to anyone working in education. Chris's accidental slip into 1961 is perhaps the best thing that could have happened to him, especially at that moment. He not only sees what the future meant for his son but is also able to use the future technically to save his son and metaphorically to save his team of California-bound pioneers. Chris Horn develops a vision after stepping only a few yards into *The Twilight Zone*. He uses that vision to save his son and renew the group's optimism.

Leaders of any school or school district who do not firmly believe in having a vision for all children under their roof will never reach the pinnacle of success that they would otherwise. Every child can succeed. There are indeed dismal facts surrounding crime, suicide, lifelong poverty, and other societal mishaps and tragedies. But without sustained optimism and an interest in working with all children, a team is never complete.

Chris Horn isn't the only *Twilight Zone* character who believes in miracles and has a vision to succeed. Charles "Charlie" Whitley from season 3, episode 21, "Kick the Can," is also a believer in the spirit of youth and the magic that's associated with one's own youth as they grow older.[2] Charlie, too, purchased a ticket for this flight, and because he had so much to talk to Chris Horn about, he sat right next to him as Passenger 6B.

Charlie spends his final days, months, or years at Sunnyvale Rest Home, a nursing home for the elderly right in the outskirts of *The Twilight Zone*. Unlike some other residents who are annoyed at the local kids playing a rudimentary game of Kick the Can on the lawns of Sunnyvale, Charlie enjoys watching them and insists that the noise they make, that constant nuisance brought to the nursing home's patients, aren't nuisances at all but rather sounds of joy, magic, and youth.

Charlie quickly catches a fever. Not a sickness, as his good friend, Ben Conroy, thinks, but the fever of being young and a little reckless. He dances in the sprinkler on the front lawn; walks around the house with energy, trying to get everyone else to get up and move around; and, finally, organizes a game of Kick the Can in the middle of the night with all the other residents. Ben refuses to join and calls him crazy for even thinking that anyone should be out of the house after dark.

Ben's opposition is felt by no one else. There is some hesitation among the others, but eventually they decide to give it a try. When the head nurse and supervisor of the home are both fast asleep, the elders put their plan into motion and start a fun game of Kick the Can outside on the lawn and in the surrounding woods. By the time Ben gets the supervisor up and goes outside with him to bring everybody back to their senses, the entire crew has gone through the reverse-aging process, all young again and playing Kick the Can. The spirit of being young again is so effective that all but one resident literally turn into children.

Rather than taking another turn into the annals of science fiction, the following events are noteworthy because they not only can change one's outlook on education, children, and personal growth but can also assuredly bring one out of that sticky time warp of a sort—trying the same methods over and over again with little or no results for students. It is not unusual for educators to find themselves in a black hole in the far reaches of outer space, being the eternal pessimist who stops creating and thinking outside the box because they're tired of getting eight to ten "failures" a year. Some educators "know" which ones will "fail" after the first three days of school.

Without optimism and pockets of success where they're seldom anticipated, some educators will feel as though they've been sentenced to hard time in an extraterrestrial POW camp teaching basic keyboarding. These are the ones who unfortunately begin counting the days until they can retire and find solace watching endless reruns of their favorite space-race captain chasing phantom UFOs somewhere beyond the clouds.

Providing a platform for others to get onto the right path in life is a vital part of any strong educator's attributes. While one could argue that the cumulative actions taken by each individual will often influence whether they are successful, educators are responsible for nurturing all students so that they can ultimately accomplish their goals. The key here is believing in every child as well as oneself, always.

Often, unexpected victories with children do more than change an individual's perception about them. They could lead to a connection that has life-altering consequences. Providing just the right amount of intrinsic motivation for both adult and student could be the fork in the road that a particular child had been seeking for years.

Take the following student athlete, Chad. Known for his lightning-like speed on the elementary playgrounds and unmatched knowledge of America's pastime, Chad had envisioned playing in the majors one day. When all his dreams were abruptly shattered after being cut from the middle school baseball team just one year after hitting a home run in the Little League playoff game, an alert teacher ended up having a side conversation with the school's track coach.

When the track coach decided to make an unexpected visit to the same student's special education class to "pick up a book," she spontaneously struck up a conversation with Chad, asking who he was and what he was doing after school. The trusted special education teacher had a very strong relationship with Chad and quickly became involved in the conversation.

It didn't last long. It didn't need to. Chad went down to the track that day and found a new interest. He had decided first to run track. He could go out for baseball the following year. But then, he ran cross-country, then in 5k races, then in marathons. The lasting impact of one alert teacher's ability to recognize when a student was down and then bring it to the attention of someone who could connect briefly with that same student and change his mind-set may have been what that student needed to move forward in athletics.

The victories stretched farther than the finish lines on various roads, dirt trails, and painted tracks. For his senior leadership project, Chad designed and built a cross-country course at a local park and organized a race for charity. The young seventh-grader who was in tears once and crushed by his dreams of possibly becoming a Major League Baseball player someday had become not only a runner but also someone who gave back to his community. Running connected Chad with school, and running is what he gave back to his community.

Other students may need to see that connection they've been waiting for in a much different way. Take Will, for instance. Will's personality: defiant. Work ethic: nonexistent. Those two traits were only observable to a novice or one who was counting the days until they're released from that extraterrestrial duty. What Will's teacher did know about him, though, was that he never did homework. In fact, he never really wrote down anything: homework, notes, essays, short answers on tests, long answers on tests.

To some, the homework really didn't matter because they knew that Will didn't seem to have a good home life. After all, he was normally disheveled when he came in as the late bell rang and was never in a hurry to get his materials ready for learning. That was acceptable to some, however, because they could adjust and differentiate things for Will. He could just be held to a different standard.

Will's social studies teacher thought that bringing in a relative who worked in a factory close to home and had to overcome poverty like other first-generation Americans had would have piqued his interest. But Will didn't really contribute to the class discussion that day or on any other day. Will's teacher knew this and didn't give up hope. Keeping true to her values and what she thought worked best for students, she created a new assignment that would allow the students to work as an individual or in pairs so that she could find some time to chat with Will and see if she could motivate him somehow.

She created a new project and assigned it to her students, giving them the last ten to fifteen minutes to gather their thoughts and ask clarifying questions if necessary. She attempted to have a conversation with Will. He spoke but really didn't provide any insight. During the following two to three days, the teacher allowed students to work on their Gilded Age projects. The objective was to create an invention for the people of that time period. It could be any person or group of people, but it had to be someone who lived and suffered somehow during the Gilded Age. The invention had to address a Gilded Age problem.

Will came to class as usual and actually had something on his desk indicative of some level of engagement. When he raised his hand to volunteer to present his invention, his teacher was figuratively floored. Will had created an invention that surpassed many in the class, but his creative thinking, hard work, and actual engagement pleasantly surpassed his teacher's expectations. Will created a suit of armor and called it Mjolnir. He not only created it in his head but had also built a prototype for a GI Joe toy doll. Mjolnir, in Will's words, was built for and marketed toward the Chinese and Irish immigrants working in the mines out West as well as the police who were fighting against the growing waves of organized crime gangs in America's larger cities.

Will earned a 100, thoroughly impressed his social studies teacher, and demonstrated that he was capable of working with the right mix of factors that interested him. His teacher took more out of the experience than she had anticipated. Will's interests *could* lie in Norse mythology, reading, action figures, or possibly action/adventure. What she did know for sure was that this particular project piqued Will's interest so much that he excelled.

The immediate effects of this incident were reaching and notable. However, the far-reaching effects were more than notable. Approximately ten years later, the same teacher and the same student were near each other in line at a local pet store. Hardly recognizable, Will struck up a conversation with his former teacher and reintroduced himself. The man that she had encountered, once seemingly unmotivated, unengaged, and troubled, was now a conversive, engaging, mature dog trainer. Beyond that, the connection that was built may not have been deep and constant, but it was borne out of a simple project and one teacher's drive to get through to a challenging student.

Not all challenging students are noticeable through academics. Take our third student, Maggie. Winter weather had extended far into the spring one year when Maggie had been navigating other treacherous obstacles. Her parents had been split for some time, but as she grew older and became a junior in high school, her father had moved out of the area and lost nearly all contact with her. It angered her, but she was used to adversity, as she had learned quickly how to navigate her mother balancing multiple daytime and evening jobs and her stepfather's chemical addictions.

When she had been sent to the in-school detention room to make up yet another test that she had missed for being out for five consecutive days, she had finally lost it. The teacher on duty called for administration, which resulted in a speedy response by the assistant principal. The assistant principal tried her best to remove Maggie from the room through coaxing, but Maggie refused to leave, choosing instead to continue with a tirade of verbal assaults and foul expletives.

The assistant principal then radioed to the principal, who responded and determined as she walked in that, if Maggie wouldn't leave the room, the other students would have to. She directed everyone out of the room and had the teacher on duty lead the other students to an open room next door. Maggie then turned her attention onto the principal and began carrying out a new onslaught of profanities aimed mainly at authority figures.

The principal recognized immediately that Maggie's anger was not being directed at her, her assistant, the teacher on duty, or the other children. She was simply angry and needed some more serious forms of intervention that the school likely couldn't provide. She kept an even tone with Maggie and allowed her to continue, methodically taking it in and responding with short, quick questions, related redirections, and validations:

"I think you need some help."

"I understand. I get it. I don't blame you for being angry."

"Do you want some help?"

"Do you want me to help?"

"I don't know what you're going through, but I can help you find some help if you want."

At some point during that short interaction between two people with very different histories, Maggie broke down and started to cry. From there, the swearing and elevated voice in the room disappeared, and some tough-to-face truths were followed by short, nurturing responses and rich periods of silence. After acknowledging what was troubling her, the principal's next strategy was simply to work on getting Maggie out of the class and into a counselor's office, where they would discuss her situation in more detail and find some help outside school.

Despite the tirade that disrupted a few test takers, the teacher on duty, and two administrators, the principal gave Maggie a break, allowing her to stay out of classes for the rest of the day, then focusing on finding the immediate assistance, and then returning when she had some coping strategies that she had a hand in developing.

The principal also recognized that the systems in place needed to be revisited. When students missed consecutive days or even one day, how much should they be expected to make up upon returning to school? A shared document with major tests and assignments building-wide was in order. So was a meeting to discuss what to do when an adult in the building recognizes a student who may be suffering from mental health issues or major familial problems.

What most educators perceive as being dysfunctional may be the norm at a student's home. Often, the home situation is at the root of their behavior, and school personnel cannot simply sweep it under the carpet because the child is doing fine at school. Rather, the mind-set should be that children in crisis—whether serious or peripheral—may act out. From there, effective leaders, whether they be administrators or teachers, need to develop strategies to address explosive behaviors and get students the help they need.

Our systems should also be built not for the student of yesteryear, who will come in and adhere to the rules, but for all students, knowing that most of them today may come from homes run by a single parent, transiency, or a fixed-income family. Furthermore, school leaders who assess situations and then address them prescriptively rather than addressing them through a strict interpretation of a student handbook will set the groundwork for building relationships with students. Once that groundwork has been established, it is the intrinsic desire for change that will motivate and lead students to self-reflect and thus grow.

PASSENGER MANIFEST

6A
Name: Chris Horn
Occupation: Pioneer; traveler
Redeeming Qualities: Develops a vision; spreads hope to team members; optimistic; takes action; takes risks; will not bow to adversity even under seemingly impossible circumstances
Atlantian Fields Usability Rating: 10/10
Leadership Potential: 10/10
Confidential Advisories: None

6B
Name: Charlie Whitely
Occupation: Retired
Redeeming Qualities: Energetic; stands up to pessimism and those who limit the potential of others; fosters a sense of freedom, independence, and strength
Atlantian Fields Usability Rating: 10/10
Leadership Potential: 10/10
Confidential Advisories: Salary will depend on Atlantian Fields retirement limits

PLANNING FOR SUCCESS: KEY IDEA

- Every child has in them not only the ability to succeed but also the abilities to shine and excel. They also have the ability to cry out and are vulnerable to having outbursts. A positive, optimistic mind-set and belief in all of them is a must for a high-quality educational leader, whether they are a teacher or building or district administrator.

PLANNING FOR SUCCESS: OTHER LEADERSHIP QUALITIES AND STRATEGIES

- The magic of youth and optimistic vision of a bright, successful future will drive many to succeed. When an educational leader shares such practices and optimism, others will follow, and a shared vision of success will permeate the organization.
- Address each child prescriptively, and do not rely on "zero-tolerance" practices.
- Do not dwell on the past or let it control how the organization progresses.
- Teachers and educational leaders may not realize when they've had an influence over a child to help them succeed, but the long-term impacts may be more important than ever realized.
- Intrinsic rewards will motivate students, teachers, and leaders and help people become successful.

REFLECTIONS FOR YOUR ORGANIZATION

- What steps are educators taking to intrinsically or extrinsically motivate students?
- Do members or the leadership team generally speak in terms of the future or the past?
- What steps are being taken to develop and share a common vision?
- How do all members of the educational team identify excellence, and are pockets of relative extraordinary success realized?
- Is the mind-set of the organization one that leads all to believe in the abilities of all children?
- How are members of the educational community building connections with all students and their guardians?

NOTES

1. Rod Serling, *The Twilight Zone*, season 2, episode 23, "A Hundred Yards over the Rim," aired April 7, 1961, on CBS.

2. Rod Serling, *The Twilight Zone*, season 3, episode 21, "Kick the Can," aired February 9, 1962, on CBS.

Chapter 7

Building Atlantian Fields School District

Most beings onboard had been sleeping for a good portion of the ship's journey through the last galaxy. The friendly voice that universally translated thousands of languages across the stars for the last century or so came over the PA system to announce that we would be heading into the nearest time-flash zone within an hour. Sil sat back, glanced at his sleeping children, shut his eyes, and didn't wake up until the ship had landed on Atlantian Fields soil.

By the time they arrived, the plutonium clean-up had been complete. New ceilo ports had been erected for safe, easy travel. Floating buildings with freshwater supplies flowing beneath them dotted the landscape. Houses riddled with every imaginable holographic energy source all rolled up into a secure device no larger than a thumbnail were readily available for occupation at historically low prices.

The need for a free public education for all children wasn't lost in time, not for any being with two, three, or ten feet. Mr. Shiner's favorite customer did find work, while Atlantian Fields took its first baby steps toward revitalization. Soon after, Sil acquired the position of superintendent of the newly formed Atlantian Fields School District. His mission: build a top universal district that produces interplanetary citizens who think progressively and have the ability to create wherever they seek to grow, settle, or make their presence positively known.

Despite having come from advancements far beyond our current prototypes, the pioneers of the redevelopment of Atlantian Fields found themselves working with children who have the same needs as those in today's society. Every single one of them is unique in their own way, but they all come in with the same common denominators: the need to grow and learn.

Needing to act swiftly with the growing population streaming in from galaxies previously unheard of, the community came together to build state-of-the-art schools outfitted with the latest technological capabilities and teaching resources. As trade and prosperity grew, so did the need for newer gadgets, alternative teaching practices, and quality leaders. It is here where our friends from Flight 607 take on new roles.

As superintendent of Atlantian Fields School, Sil worked tirelessly to put a team together with members whose strengths complimented one another's. The Atlantian Fields School District was established with three distinct buildings: an elementary school (K–5), a middle school (6–8), and a high school (9–12). In order to allow for a firm foundational setting, the Atlantian Fields leadership team must believe in growing every single child every day.

For this reason, Sil and the board of education will work together to find the most highly qualified leaders to help the children of Atlantian Fields step into their future. Each and every child coming to Atlantian Fields School District must feel safe. Children cannot maximize their learning experience if they do not feel safe in their environment. For that reason, it is essential that the district create a head of security. This leader's role includes but is not limited to facilitating and directing safety measures on all school grounds and all transportation vehicles managed by the district; fostering a supportive relationship with staff, students, and the community; and taking the lead on all safety drills and procedures.

It is crucial that this leader create and maintain open lines of communication, foster transparency, and design formal procedures to settle disputes with sustainable and positive outcomes. The right person for this position will also be one who can form bonds with all parents, guardians, local business owners, and community advocates in order to promote a community mind-set. The Atlantian Fields community feels strongly about modeling for their children. When each one graduates from Atlantian Fields High School, they will be on a pathway toward success with a safe, law-abiding, community-oriented mind-set.

For this position, Sil and his team have chosen Mr. Chambers from "To Serve Man." While Mr. Chambers let his guard down and ended up putting his own life as well as the lives of others at risk, he was, at one point in time, a member of a US federal intelligence agency. This experience cannot go unnoticed. Furthermore, the team had a growth mind-set that values all people. Too often, when a storm hits, people tend to point their fingers and blame others. However, teams of leaders are often hampered by a state of complacency. They aren't expecting the unexpected. People who make mistakes but otherwise have a strong work history deserve second chances.

As a free, democratic society, we have traversed miles of treacherous terrain covering crime and punishment as well as rehabilitation. Clearly, there are still hardened criminals and people with unsolvable mental health disorders whose riddles we have not yet been able to crack. However, the Atlantian Fields leadership team does not label people for the rest of their lives unless they clearly present a danger to others.

Mr. Chambers himself will be charged with putting his own security team together, complete with appropriate audiovisual equipment, building safety design and details, and communication devices. But equipment, design, technology, and other materials will not suffice when it comes to truly securing a school district's campuses. Mr. Chambers's best asset is his ability to build and maintain relationships. In the episode "To Serve Man," he was a part of a team that was granted authority over translating a book left behind by a Kanamit. The military generals who worked with Mr. Chambers trusted his judgment, despite some of his backhanded humorous comments toward them.

He maintained his professionalism throughout the ordeal and had a trustworthy team of professionals working with him to crack the code, so to speak, of the Kanamit language. When the task was finally complete, it was Mr. Chambers's assistant who ran through the airport, screaming at him not to board the ship bound for the Kanamits' planet. The team had completed their interpretation of the book, and she tried desperately to prevent Mr. Chambers—her team's leader—from meeting the same fate as several American turkeys do every November.

The loyalty and dedication not only to completing the task on hand, despite doing it against seemingly impossible odds, is precisely the kind of culture that Sil and the team would like him to build in the Atlantian Fields School District. This choice wasn't easy, and some were opposed.

Active community member and board watcher Olaf Harriman was more than hesitant to support this choice. He maintained that he firmly believed in giving people second chances, and with the Kanamit's cover blown, he knew that there was no longer a looming threat to turn men into meals. His discomfort was primarily caused by the fact that Mr. Chambers once worked in the federal government of the United States. He didn't have any experience with school security.

While this could certainly raise the ire of any public figure representing the people or anyone competing for the same position, Sil and the board of education chose Mr. Chambers for his people skills and strong work ethic. Taking someone slightly out of their element and putting them into a related position that requires an aligned knowledge base was something that they saw as an opportunity. In their opinion, Mr. Chambers had something to learn as a school employee, and his eagerness to apply for the job was, also in their opinion, a factor that would allow both him and the school to grow together.

Furthermore, they concluded and relayed to Mr. Harriman that Mr. Chambers would not be alone in creating and maintaining campus security. Everyone in the learning community has a role: faculty, staff, and students. The team is only as good as its own eyes and ears. Mr. Chambers will be working side by side with Sil, as will the district's fiscal leader. Fiscal responsibility is something that is expected from local, state, and federal governmental representatives. This is no different from what is expected in schools. Increased budgets are a natural part of growth in any society. However, they do not always yield better results.

As a new, upcoming district with a growing population and great deal of potential, it would be nothing short of insanity to hire somebody who didn't have some working knowledge of managing a community's pot of money. For this reason, Sil and his team hired the former superintendent of Tall Carnivorous Oaks School District. Not only will she be the lead on budgeting and financial matters, but she will also take the lead on personnel. She has already proven to be effective in working with building leaders, district leaders, the board of education, community members, parents, and students.

Remember that she started with very targeted meetings with all her leaders in every realm of the district. She followed up by putting together a responsible budget free of unnecessary expenses and unsustainable resources. She kept the dismal fiscal reality of the situation in the forefront of her meetings and balanced the community's needs with what it could support. All employees who were going to lose their jobs at the end of that fiscal year were brought in for an honest face-to-face conversation with the superintendent and their immediate supervisor. Counseling resources and information on other districts or organizations that might be hiring were also offered to each employee, as were the parameters for call backs and benefits granted through unemployment.

When the budget was proposed, she set the stage for large, lengthy meetings with the sole purpose of allowing everyone who wanted to voice their support or opposition to speak. In her new position, director of finance and personnel, she will be working proactively to secure monies from various sources in order to avoid having to make drastic cuts or large tax increases that the community may not be able to handle in the future.

Her first order of business in growing Atlantian Fields School District was putting together a series of schedules that allowed the district to minimize employee idleness and maximize all its resources, including professional staff. A staggered starting time for all buildings was implemented so that shared staff could be used in multiple places and at multiple times. She also ushered in preventative maintenance on everything from each school's infrastructure to the pods used to transport students.

Keeping in mind that her roots lie in fostering ways to allow children to succeed, her most unique implementation now is a high school schedule that allowed for flexibility in on-site student attendance based on evidence that they are learning and growing. She worked closely with the high school principal on building such a schedule that saves on money, maximizes student performance, and is more closely aligned with the professional work community. More detail will follow when we read about the set-up of Atlantian Fields High School.

Each school building in the Atlantian Fields School District will undoubtedly develop its own culture as it nurtures its youth and prepares them for an uncertain but optimistic future. There are, however, a certain set of ground rules or parameters built into each school's culture from the beginning. They are nonnegotiable and aligned with the Atlantian Fields School District's mission of building a top universal district producing interplanetary citizens who think progressively and have the ability to create wherever they seek to grow, settle, or make their presence positively known.

The values of every leader in the Atlantian Fields School District are repeated in ceremonial fashion after each one of them signs his or her contract:

- We believe in each and every child every day.
- We take a nurturing approach to guidance and conflict resolution.
- We are a team. We take a team approach to problem solving, and we maintain an out-of-the-box style of thinking. Without teams, progress is delayed or completely stifled.
- We believe that improvement is constant and that setbacks are a natural, unavoidable part of the improvement process.
- There is no one-size-fits-all mentality or standard for educating children.
- Some students will not engage in a traditional setting.
- Every decision made on any given day could have unintended consequences. All decisions should be made with ripple effects in mind.
- People deserve second chances, and it is within our community mentality that we allow for each other to learn from our mistakes.

The mission is the philosophical hinge that fastens each decision to the district's core belief. The roadmap for accomplishing that mission must include goals for each level so that the dipstick that checks the plasma in each ceilocart's engine can tell every driver if they are on track or traversing uncharted, dead-end dirt roads.

For that reason, the Atlantian Fields Board of Education, in conjunction with Superintendent Sil, organized open work sessions, announced well in advance, to create measurable goals for each school. By the time each child exits

- Supersonic Elementary School, they will be able to read and write at a sixth-grade level or higher, as evidenced by their performance on a series of aligned tasks at various points in the school year;
- Cosmic Way Middle School, they will be able to earn at least one credit in a high-school-level course and demonstrate literacy in each of the core subject areas through verbal and visual presentation of a finished product;
- Atlantian Fields High School, they will graduate with a diploma sufficient for acceptance into a postsecondary education organization

or institute, be exposed to a college-level curriculum for at least one high school course, and gain experience in a professional work setting off campus through an apprenticeship, internship, job shadowing, or being an active member of the workforce.

SUPERSONIC ELEMENTARY SCHOOL

Nurturing, reading, writing, self-esteem, enjoyment, friendship, love, make-believe, creativity, art, music. These are the first words that should come to one's mind upon entering Supersonic Elementary School in Atlantian Fields. The signs, student work, ways in which visitors are greeted, smiles, choice of verbiage should all conjure up images of all these words no matter what day of the school year it is.

Some children come from backgrounds that many educators wouldn't even have nightmares about. They come from poverty, physically or sexually abusive guardians, homes where the electricity or gas has been turned off, and shared bedrooms and living quarters. They come with unknown or undiagnosed mental health issues, in fear, with anxiety, scared, and alone.

But they come. And because of that, they are to be held, helped, led, and educated. None of them—no matter how scared or scary, fearing or fearful, abused or abusive—is as evil, conniving, and destructive, as Anthony Fremont appeared to be. For that reason, Sil chose passenger 5B, Ms. Helen Foley, from Spielberg's *Twilight Zone* remake of "It's a Good Life," to lead Supersonic Elementary School. Ms. Foley's natural ability to care and develop a partnership that presumably enabled a monster child to openly admit his desire for companionship and direction cannot be underestimated. If she could do with other kids or every kid what she did with Anthony, she is undoubtedly the one to lead others to do the same.

Ms. Foley will put a system into place that embraces diversity, the downtrodden, and every mental health disorder that comes her way. Ms. Foley will stand back while being in the middle, analyze, think, then execute. Ms. Foley will lead by example with the parents; staff; and, most importantly, the children. Her best quality: She's an agent of change. Helen Foley singlehandedly brought the monster who terrorized and controlled Peaksville for years to his knees. She did this not by force but through a set of skills that one can only develop through wisdom and experience.

To be such an agent and lead such change, one must embrace the concept of seeing the potential in people and giving them second chances. This fundamental core belief is essential for anyone working with children. For those who are at the elementary level, it is crucial for them to not only see this but to live and learn it, as well.

When working with parents of children who make pretty bad decisions on school grounds, keep in mind that not every child is so easily influenced at that age. A poverty-stricken home life can certainly overshadow the care of even the most nurturing teacher. In elementary school, many children see a parent or guardian or sitter every day when they wake up and every night when they go to bed. That constant must be a positive influence on each of their lives, regardless of what their socioeconomic status is.

Unconditional love. It must be present. Because it isn't always, it is up to Ms. Helen Foley to spread her influence into every corner of the district that sends children to her. It is for that reason that every student attending Supersonic Elementary School has an in-person meeting with Principal Foley, either at school or at home. The purpose of such a meeting is to have a face-to-face conversation about each child's behavioral, academic, and social goals. It is here where Ms. Foley will connect with parents and convey to them the ways in which they can partner with the school to help each child achieve their goals.

Finally, Ms. Foley will implement what she has herself dubbed "CROW." Crows. Not a very colorful creature. Certainly not too terribly intriguing either. But crows they are at Supersonic Elementary School, so much so that crows adorn the hallways, sit perched atop trees that suck in the sunlight in the main lobby, visit classrooms randomly to check on each worm's progress, and are incorporated into every piece of communication that goes out to parents and/or students. The kids have come to love crows and no longer take them for granted when playing outside or traversing the countryside in their ceilocarts.

Why crows? Ms. Foley is not only the principal but also the founder of the program that she was charged with creating soon after she was hired, and that is CROW: Create, Read, Originate, Write. Every cumulative assignment and assessment begin with the word *create*. Atlantian Fields wants their students to be creative thinkers. They want them to reach for originality, to be the pioneers of an unpredictable future. They want them to be able to expect the unexpected.

The next step in the process is to read. Each child should read for a purpose, and every cumulative assignment carries with it a set of given resources that will be helpful for completing the task on hand. However, each assignment will also allow for students to find resources of their own and read whatever noteworthy information they contain with the purpose of completing the task.

Too often, kids do not want to read. So the phrase *reading for a purpose* became commonplace. The problem that often exists is the purpose. Kids do not often see it. In Supersonic Elementary School, they truly are reading for a purpose because they are engaged. When they're not engaged, it's the teacher's job to partner with them and their guardians to find ways to get them engaged.

The next component of each CROW assessment—the *O*—is the most important: Originate. Students are to use their mind, insight, creativity, resources, knowledge, and artistic side to develop an original final product that they submit for a grade. Each of these incorporates concepts from mathematics and either science or social studies or both.

Grammatical elements may also be assessed, but most of the language assessment comes from the fourth letter, *W*, standing for *write*. Handed in with each assignment is a written summary of what it is and how its creator went about completing their task. Each summary must contain both facts and opinions as well as a cited list of resources.

The following is an example from one of Ms. Foley's fifth-grade classrooms:

Task: Create any type of park in a vacant lot of your choice found anywhere in or near Atlantian Fields. It should take no more than forty minutes to get there by ceilocart, and you must use existing travel ways.

Your park should:

- include at least three things that will attract people of any age to it,
- be large enough to include parking and charging stations for ceilocarts,
- have clear dimensions for each section of it, and
- be advertised creatively through any modern means of communication.

You may work with up to two partners for this project, and your team will have two in-class days to work on it. The rest should be completed outside class. Communication with other teams and individuals is essential because your park must be one of a kind.

Each group and individual will present their park along with their advertisement and written summary/response on Friday. Be prepared to answer questions from both the teacher and your peers. Questions may be related to the time it takes to travel to your park, the variety of people who would be attracted to your park, or the dimensions of each feature found in your park.

There are several key components to this sample assignment:

- It is highly engaging and hands-on. Or it is highly engaging *because* it is hands-on.
- It will incorporate real-life mathematical skills as well as ELA skills and possibly both science and social studies concepts.
- Students will work in teams.
- Students will not only use resources but also be positioned to find resources.
- Students will be positioned to answer questions posed by their peers and their teacher and therefore will have to think on their three feet.
- Students will acquire public-speaking and presentation skills.

Most students tend to go to kindergarten and many other grade levels with some degree of anxiety. There is nothing wrong with that. A great deal of overwhelming untreated anxiety, however, can become extremely prohibitive by the time students get into the middle-level grades. Therefore, it is essential that all teachers at Supersonic Elementary School nurture and love each and every child as if they are their own.

These two vital functions will lead to trust and respect for all students and among all students. Fear of the unknown, of looking stupid in front of others, of large crowds, and of social situations needs to be addressed and overcome. Students at Supersonic Elementary School lead and present with and for each other at each grade level and take this skill set and any other skill set that evolves into the next level of education.

COSMIC WAY MIDDLE SCHOOL

The essential components of any strong lesson include student engagement, the use of supporting information for solving a problem or completing a task, and a student-centered/student-guided body. Strong hooks and closures are certainly crucial when it comes to student engagement and "dipsticking" progress. But those two alone can't make a strong lesson when the other components are lacking.

The teacher-centered stand-and-deliver method is long gone in terms of capturing every student and really getting each one to learn. This is not as prevalent at the elementary level nowadays, but the middle schools are not immune to it. At times, middle school leaders embrace the mind-set that they are getting their students "prepared for high school."

The middle school years could be the most crucial ones in defining a child, with such a wide range of physical, social, emotional, and maturity levels. Middle school should not be an extension of elementary school. Nor should it be an introduction to high school. It should be what it is: middle school.

Middle schools often consist of teams of teachers, one per core subject area as well as one special education teacher. Whether these exist in Cosmic Way Middle School or not, the concept of a team of teachers supporting teams of students is a good one. At Cosmic Way, each student is paired with a teacher in the building for mentoring and support with everything, from getting involved in extracurricular activities to friendship woes. The social and emotional well-being of each child at Cosmic Way is just as important as their academic well-being. That mentality is what has led to the academic foundation and leadership team of Cosmic Way Middle School.

To lead Cosmic Way Middle School, one must possess a unique set of skills and personality traits that jive with the middle school mind. Many students are still invincible, having no fear of nearly anything that would be sensationalized on social media, while others still sneak into their parents' beds at night for fear of the oversized monsters who somehow manage to lurk underneath their bedroom carpet.

Many of them will grow to the point of no longer being recognizable, while others will look as young as they did at Supersonic Elementary School. Many will be bold enough to run for class president and know that they'll secure votes based on their popularity, while others won't even know what a class president does. The differences at the middle level are far and wide, and everyone working at a middle school must recognize that. Who better to lead such a grassroots effort as Atlantian Fields is revitalized? None other than Passengers 6A and 6B: Chris Horn and Charlie Whitley.

Both men were not only adamant but also very convincing in their drive to lead their team and totally reverse that team's mind-set. The objects for each one helped immensely: the penicillin for Chris Horn and a magical tin can for Charles Whitley. However, neither would have been useful if the spirit for each leader wasn't there. Each of them was influenced by children, and that contagious youthful energy provided them with the fortitude to tackle a problem and seek to reverse course for their benefit as well as the benefits of others.

Furthermore, these two gentlemen proved that they are capable of putting teams together against insurmountable odds. They have an end in mind and are convincing not only with their words but with their actions, as well. They model what they want others to do so that the team is cohesive and integrated. The leaders themselves are a part of the change that they are creating.

Traditionally, middle school teams have included a special education teacher, core class subject teachers, and perhaps a specialized encore subject teacher. Too often, large teams with the same people working together month after month and year after year become complacent. At Cosmic Way Middle School, it is up to the teachers and leaders to develop teams designed to address the ongoing issues that surface during the school year. These teams could be considered internal auditors of Cosmic Way's academic programs.

Each of the academic programs here also revolve around the concept of teams. The teachers, administrators, and other personnel work in teams, and it should be the case with all students at Cosmic Way. Developing strong, student-centered, project-based assessments is the norm, not the exception, here at Cosmic Way. This does not mean that students work together for the purpose of having a buddy or friend to help them along academically. What it does mean is that at Cosmic Way, teachers create lessons that are challenging enough so that students need to work together to complete a task.

An example of such teamwork combined with an ongoing issue and challenging task is as follows:

1. 70 percent of seventh-grade male students are having difficulties with answering extended written-response science questions as evidenced by the results of four assessments administered by Mrs. Pewter through the first three units of study.
   - Mrs. Pewter has gathered the evidence and sought help from several English teachers.
   - Mrs. Bee finds that a portion of these same male students are also having a difficult time recalling information that she's taught though her first units of study.
   - The two form a team and bring in Special Education Teacher Gail Papa for assistance.
   - Each student's work is analyzed, patterns are identified, and new methods of teaching "extended relevant written responses" are taught.
   - New assessments are put into place, combining the elements of teamwork, constructivism, the content, and an extended written response.
   - Creativity and rigor are put into place.
   - Final product: a task in which students work in pairs to present verbally using a scripted conversation between a frog and leopard comparing notes on how their bodily systems have evolved in order to survive in their respective climates.

Certainly, a lesson like this could be adapted to almost any subject—two historical figures discussing the differences between their motives for fighting in a war or two different math laws having a conversation on why they are essential to understanding certain mathematical principles—and used at nearly every level.

At the middle level, however, too many students go through that awkward stage of growing too quickly or too slowly, and it affects them socially. Having fun with academics through social activity and a strong foundational set of rigorous expectations will allow for students to see the support and interdependency of each other while giving them confidence to help their peers.

Under the Confucius model of interdependency, friend-to-friend relationships should be at the core of every middle school program decision. This is the place where we as a society "lose" a number of kids—not literally, but academically. It is time to change the mind-set of the middle school leader, teacher, and student.

ATLANTIAN FIELDS HIGH SCHOOL

According to the National Center for Educational Statistics, the high school graduation rate in 2019 was 86 percent.[1] In Atlantian Fields, like the United States of America, every student will be educated, freely and appropriately, until they have aged out. They will not give up on any student.

With all the publicity and high-stakes performances associated with high schools across the country, our best-suited passenger for this job is none other than the "misfit" toy major from "Five Characters in Search of an Exit." The major's proactive, no-excuse, no-obstacle-is-too-big approach combined with his contagious energy and simple, in-plain-sight, convincing explanations are qualities that all high school leaders should possess in order to move their team forward with a vision of success. The major had one goal in the classic *Twilight Zone* episode: to get out of the cage they were living in. Within the confines of the short TV drama, he was able to use wisdom, limited resources, and mind-set to change the complacency of every single other misfit toy in the barrel. Even after the first attempt at escape failed, the team tried again with an alternate approach.

Despite their efforts, the toys stayed confined for the time being. That is until they were "rescued" by underprivileged children who could give them the love, identity, and freedom they were seeking. That part the viewer never sees. However, viewers are certainly left not only with an aha moment of who these random strangers were and how they ended up in that circular pen but also with a glimmer of hope that they will eventually be given to a child and provided with a new home.

In addition to changing everyone else's mind-set, the major employs strategies crucial to pushing the team toward success. First, he develops his team. Their collective mind-set was one of complacency. Among other lines, the clown acknowledges that things were easier before the major had arrived. One by one, each character changes his or her mind-set as the major pushes forward through seemingly insurmountable obstacles. Once their mind-set is changed, he develops the team. The most indignant of them all—the clown—is the last one to be convinced, but through positive peer influence, he comes around and joins the team in their quest to search for an exit.

The next thing the major does: He builds trust. At the first attempt to escape, the major places himself at the base of the human ladder, carrying all the weight of the other four characters on his shoulders. When that fails, he determines that he will be the one climbing to the top and escaping, all the while convincing all of them that he will be back for them. Finally, he creates. He creates with his mind and uses the team's limited resources—a broken sword, scraps of their clothing, and their own physical strength—to scale the wall.

At Atlantian Fields High School, the major employs these same strategies. Some teachers are complacent. He uses logic and a changed mind-set of other teacher leaders to move the mind-sets of the complacent teachers. This is done through his PD initiatives. For each scheduled faculty meeting, teachers have a range of choices. They can work together in a small group designed specifically to overcome a challenging obstacle related to student learning or attend any one of a handful of "best practices" presentations being offered at the same time.

The major also maintains trust at Atlantian Fields High School. He is honest and straightforward with his staff through various practices. He has an open-door approach, fielding questions, giving advice, and maintaining confidentiality when it comes to everything from formal evaluations to personal issues. He also puts people into positions of leadership based on their abilities and skills, careful not to choose the same people over and over again. Through his PD, best practices, and teacher-guided team initiatives, it is a part of the culture that there isn't a watchful eye in the sky distrusting everyone's professional integrity. Rather, teachers know they are trusted, as is their leader.

Trustworthiness doesn't stop within the doors of Atlantian Fields High School. When working with students, the major is open to reasonable suggestions on everything from disciplinary consequences to starting a new club. When suspending students, for instance, the major will work with both the suspended child and their parent(s) in order to not only make sure the consequence is just but also that the child gets appropriate help so that they learn from their mistakes. Every decision that ends in a student disciplinary consequence is seen as a mistake.

The major also takes the initiative to build his community: that is, a high school learning community. Parents are given the opportunity to weigh in on major changes that could affect their children. They provide suggestions through various means anytime throughout the year. Every parent is given an equal voice, yet they understand that the building principal often has to make decisions that they aren't always going to be happy with. Furthermore, many of the major's initiatives incorporate the entire building and are directly tied to the building and district's measurable academic goals.

For instance, on the annual Atlantian Fields College Prep Day, all students at every grade level who are capable of attending college or the military after high school participate. No one is left out, and parents know this ahead of time. One of the major's beliefs is that the mind-set of the community should be aligned with the mind-set of the educational team.

Perhaps the major's greatest strength as Atlantian Fields's high school leader is his ability to create. Among his attributes are creative master scheduling, finding unique ways of incorporating academic intervention services for students at risk of not meeting local standards, and developing alternative methods for students to earn credit while maintaining the rigor of the Atlantian Fields's curriculum. The major also realizes that his students will strive for excellence and create goals for their future. Unfortunately, Atlantian Fields High School has a limited number of teachers and course offerings.

With the major's creative and open mind-set, he has linked his students with elective courses that align with his master schedule time slots from other schools across other newly established communities. Like Atlantian Fields, other schools work with their parents and boards of education to write agreements with each other and pick up as many costs as possible.

The major has worked feverishly with his superintendent and the community that he helped build to totally change the way the residents of Atlantian Fields view high school. Students here have shorter summer breaks with flexible weekly schedules. The standard is that students move on to their next academic challenge based on the acquisition of skills and knowledge rather than successful completion of a numeric grade level, such as ninth grade, every June.

Teachers at Atlantian Fields also subscribe to a model of student learning based on finished projects. All students—grades 9–12—work in teams to complete challenging, rigorous tasks that require them to demonstrate progress toward proficiency or mastery in content and analytical, judgmental, and developmental skills. Some tasks incorporate a single subject matter, but most are interdisciplinary.

Students at Atlantian Fields High School are just like our students today: They aren't perfect and have the potential to be challenging and, in rarer cases, combative. Still, they are children. Everyone's task in Atlantian Fields High School is to raise the children academically and provide the most nurturing learning community possible. Acts of compassion are celebrated and recognized when appropriate. Annually, the counseling leadership team reviews the numbers of students not involved in clubs, activities, or athletics and searches for ways to connect those same students to school. Every student-related adverse situation is met with a serious response without anger or sarcasm. All professionals in the building model exactly what they expect their students to be learning.

PLANNING FOR SUCCESS: KEY IDEA

- Putting key people with highly favorable traits and/or experiences with children *and* the school community's expectations into positions of leadership will lead to a strong, stable, progressive learning environment with the parameters to successfully educate students.

PLANNING FOR SUCCESS: OTHER QUALITIES AND STRATEGIES

- A leader with a growth mind-set who values people will also value experience and the ability to learn from others as well as their own mistakes.
- People deserve second chances.

- Both safety and security are the responsibility of everyone in an organization.
- A team mind-set of togetherness will build trust and open lines of communication.
- Loyalty to a team leader is evident even when the team leader is not directly presiding over an endeavor.
- A strong team will continue to work toward a goal when they believe in their mission.
- Leaders who value others with people skills instill confidence in those whom they choose to help carry out their mission.
- Effective leaders value the experience of a proven leader or colleague, especially one who has demonstrated success under seemingly impossible circumstances.
- Reading, writing, creating, and presenting are essential skills that will build confidence and help students as they proceed through school and eventually in a professional setting.

REFLECTIONS FOR YOUR ORGANIZATION

- What qualities do you possess?
- What qualities and experiences do you value in your leaders?
- What essential skills and expectations are highlighted in your curricula, and are they universally prevalent in all subjects in your building or grade level?
- How does your school define success?
- How does your school foster the drive for all students to succeed and excel?

NOTE

1. US Department of Education. Institute of Education Sciences, National Center for Education Statistics. 2020. Fast Facts. 2021. https://nces.ed.gov/fastfacts/display.asp?id=805.

Chapter 8

Creators of Our Universe: Adopt and Adapt

Despite which staff members under any schoolhouse roof have the best intentions, educational leaders need to embrace the concept of growth and how to go about implementing improvements. Any major program, logistical change, or major shift in philosophy or mind-set that affects a whole building or district and is expected to change the relative comfort zone of all or most stakeholders needs to be visible to everyone and affect everyone, evenly or unevenly.

Education is an art. Statistics and data can be found, analyzed, used, and disseminated. However, the added value of human relationships in any educational organization will far outweigh anything that a canned formula could offer for children. Anyone working with children in any capacity needs to value their artistic qualities.

To those who are not educators and do not work with children, the ability to pinpoint an underlying issue and enact effective change may seem like challenging but very doable tasks. When those same problem solvers weigh in on educationally related issues, finding and implementing sustainable solutions is far more challenging than simply using numbers and data.

Solving the riddles of effectively leading and educating our youth is about as easy as understanding the unobtrusively evasive weird couple next door. They walk the track every morning school is not in session. They force themselves to say hello but do so with a grin about as genuine as the teenage vampire who offers to babysit their neighbor's pet snake for a few hours so that the neighbor themselves can go out to dinner. Their appearance is reasonably normal. Their mannerisms, a shade darker than transparent.

In short, there is something odd that can't quite be identified. Suddenly, it becomes clear. They have two legs, all the necessary organs for survival, and live and breathe in a house, neighborhood, town, just like most of the rest of society. They have average, run-of-the-mill jobs and eat the same foods as everyone else when they go through the drive-through lines. They go home after an unannounced visit and a few glasses of wine, only to unzip their human skin and contact the mother ship by twisting the TV antennae and tuning into the otherwise squiggly-lined Channel 6. They get behind closed doors and nestle in the privacy and security of their own home. Then, they get ready for a short hibernation.

It is then when it is realized that no one has any idea what they are. They resemble something between an upright walrus and a gecko, speak a foreign tongue that no linguists near or far can interpret, and generally like everyone else to stay at more than an arm's length away. That weird couple can play the role of everyday, ordinary citizens, but they won't know the first thing to do when put into a classroom of needy first-graders; have to resolve a conflict between two different cliques of ninth-graders; or figure out how to get little Bobby, already in sixth grade, to stop wetting his bed.

Those who teach for the right reasons are the ones who can, do, and will continue to implement change and bring sustainable improvements to the profession. Those educators who lead will do the same on a much broader scale. Very few, however, are so unique that their tried methods of working with children are as safe as a buried time capsule in a crater on the unexplored side of the moon.

One of the passengers who boarded Flight 607 to Atlantian Fields late was Passenger 8A, Mr. Salvadore Ross. Mr. Ross joined the flight in an effort to start over, similar to others whose actions forced them into a dismally unpleasant sort of purgatory. Mr. Ross joined from episode 16 of season 5, "The Self-Improvement of Salvadore Ross."[1]

Prior to boarding this flight, Mr. Ross was an arrogant twenty-something-year-old man who had one goal in mind: to win the affection of a young lady whose feelings did not reciprocate his. Neither she nor her father, who was familiar with Salvadore, could fathom the idea of the two of them together. Salvadore boarded not because of his effective use of adopting and adapting to change but because of his ineffective use of both.

While traveling through this particular episode, Mr. Ross injures his hand in a fit of rage. He ends up in a hospital room in a severe amount of pain and strikes up a conversation with an older gentleman in the same room with flulike symptoms. The two of them discuss each other's ailments, and Mr. Ross sarcastically gripes about the severity of his injury, telling his neighbor that he would love to switch problems and take on the cold rather than the presumably broken hand.

The neighbor laughingly agrees, and by morning, Salvadore and the patient with the cold miraculously switch ailments. Salvadore quickly realizes that he could switch characteristics with nearly anyone he meets. From there, Mr. Salvadore Ross cuts a series of shady deals with other people whom he comes in contact with, getting something that he wants each step of the way. He becomes wealthy and physically attractive and somehow manages to bargain away everything that would have worked against him in winning her love, including his previously bargained old age.

When Salvadore Ross finally gets to take the woman that he wants to win out on a date, she informs him that the one thing that he lacks is the compassion that a man such as her father has for her. This convinces Salvadore that he must make one final deal: to trade whatever it takes for her father's compassion.

Without seeing how Salvadore does this, the viewer is brought to a fairly happy scene between Salvadore and the woman whose affection he finally wins. After winning her and realizing that he has some explaining and apologizing to do with her father, Salvadore approaches him for one last conversation. Rather than striking a deal with him—which he does not need to do—Salvadore begins apologizing. However, the compassion that he had bargained for was no longer a part of her father's genetic makeup, and he chooses to tell Salvadore this right before he shoots him dead. In short, Mr. Salvadore Ross does not have what it takes to win the heart of his lifelong "love." Rather, he goes through life making shady deal after shady deal and doing what he has to do to "win" what he wants more than anything.

Mr. Salvadore Ross, as it turns out, does play a role here on Flight 607. Strong leaders have what it takes to build a team, make deals and bargains that work in everyone's favor, provide nurturing and positive reinforcement to others, bring a community together, and win the hearts of many. Mr. Ross, while not doing any of the above, indeed employs strategies that are noteworthy.

Throughout the episode, he adopts what he wants through those agreed-upon deals and then adapts himself to get closer to his prize. Mr. Ross is clearly one whose strategies fall short of good judgment. His personality, history, and lack of true compassion are missing the entire time. Rather than changing who he is through internal reflection and strength, Mr. Ross simply bargains for character traits and resources that he thinks he can use to buy someone else's love.

Strong leaders will employ a variety of strategies and adopt ideas from others. They will then analyze those ideas, whether they are in the form of a program implementation, technology, evaluation strategy, attendance policy, or any other new idea to improve the educational experience for their students. They will then use some parts or an alternate form of those ideas, adapting them to suit the needs of their own building or district.

However, the most noteworthy attribute of anything that is adopted or borrowed and then adapted, adjusted, or changed is not what it is but how compassionate the leader is in implementing that change. As anyone learns through this episode, true compassion will lead to powerful connections and new relationships. Those leaders who have a true passion for change and improvement will see their hard work pay off. However, they must self-reflect and grow while adopting new ideas and adapting to the continuous needs of their organization.

Whether it is in a pioneering district like Atlantian Fields or somewhere a little closer to home, every educational leader can be the model whom students, staff, and guardians not only look up to but also follow. They won't follow those who have made the same mistakes as some of our passengers, but they certainly can learn from them.

Dotting many of these once-charted and now nearly abandoned dirt roads in the surrounding countryside of Atlantian Fields are signs of life. Lost travelers may come across a stray rabbit, old tombstone, or barking dog. They'll stop their cars to ask for directions at the first sign of movement they see. They'll step out into the heat, pat the sweat from their foreheads with their handkerchiefs, and make sure their keys are ready in case zombies happen to exit the nearly collapsed wooden shacks just within eyesight. These roads are seemingly treacherous and with good reason. But all of them will, if they already do not, lie within a school district. And they, too, will need strong leaders.

Many school leaders are short-timers. Others become local legends. In either case, those who are effective are remembered not only as leaders but also movers, shakers, motivators, and good people. They will develop their own strategies and skill sets. At their core, however, they must truly love working with children. They will come from all walks of life, but that child-centered/child-growth mind-set is the glue that binds them to effective educational leadership. Like our educational community today, they've been plucked from the classroom, other positions of leadership, and out of places some wouldn't have ever thought of exploring.

When the common denominator is working with children, the keys to success at every level of educational leadership include keeping the professional team in a growth mind-set, being trustworthy, building community, creating, living empathetically and compassionately, and believing in the "magic" of every child every day. Collectively, these action steps create a firm foundation for the continuous construction of sustainably positive relationships with multiple people. The relationships, once formed, will become the skeleton from which the children, staff, community, and educational leaders will grow.

The size of any team that one works with will certainly be a factor in the speed and efficiency through which one can enact change. But no team is too small or too slow to make a difference for any one child whose support system consists solely of that educational group. When the leader or leaders of that team have the artistic ability to effectively provide for that child, a difference will be made.

PASSENGER MANIFEST

8A
Name: Salvadore Ross
Occupation: Varied
Redeeming Qualities: Can adapt and adjust to numerous situations in order to achieve his goal
Atlantian Fields Usability Rating: 3/10
Leadership Potential: 1/10
Confidential Advisories: Self-serving; lacks compassion

NOTE

1. Rod Serling, *The Twilight Zone*, season 5, episode 16, "The Self-Improvement of Salvadore Ross," aired January 17, 1964, on CBS.

Bibliography

Dante, Joe, John Landis, George Miller, and Steven Spielberg, dirs. *Twilight Zone: The Movie*. Burbank, CA: Warner Brothers, 1983.

Knight, Damon. "To Serve Man." *Galaxy of Science Fiction*, November 1950.

Seastrom, M., Chapman, C., Stillwell, R., McGrath, D., Peltola, P., Dinkes, R., and Xu, Z. 2006. User's Guide to Computing High School Graduation Rates, Volume 2: Technical Evaluation of Proxy Graduation Indicators. NCES 2006605 Common Core of Data (CCD). https://nces.ed.gov/pubsearch/pubsinfo.asp?pubid=2006605.

Serling, Rod. *The Twilight Zone*. Season 1, episode 22, "The Monsters Are Due on Maple Street." Aired March 4, 1960, on CBS.

Serling, Rod. *The Twilight Zone*. Season 2, episode 23, "A Hundred Yards over the Rim." Aired April 7, 1961, on CBS.

Serling, Rod. *The Twilight Zone*. Season 2, episode 29, "The Obsolete Man." Aired June 2, 1961, on CBS.

Serling, Rod. *The Twilight Zone*. Season 3, episode 8, "It's a Good Life." Aired November 3, 1961, on CBS.

Serling, Rod. *The Twilight Zone*. Season 3, episode 14, "Five Characters in Search of an Exit." Aired December 22, 1961, on CBS.

Serling, Rod. *The Twilight Zone*. Season 3, episode 21, "Kick the Can." Aired February 9, 1962, on CBS.

Serling, Rod. *The Twilight Zone*. Season 3, episode 24, "To Serve Man." Aired March 2, 1962, on CBS.

Serling, Rod. *The Twilight Zone*. Season 5, episode 16, "The Self-Improvement of Salvadore Ross." Aired January 17, 1964, on CBS.

US Department of Education. Institute of Education Sciences, National Center for Education Statistics. 2020. Fast Facts. 2021. https://nces.ed.gov/fastfacts/display.asp?id=805.

www.ingramcontent.com/pod-product-compliance
Lightning Source LLC
Chambersburg PA
CBHW032030230426
43671CB00005B/270